Praise for *The Truth About Organic Gardening:*

"Destined to be a bestseller....An easy to read, practical, and fascinating book."

—*Cleveland Plain Dealer*

"How do you separate the hype from the facts? Spending 13 bucks on Gillman's new book…may go a long way."

—*The Washington Post*

"The main thrust of Gillman's book is to advise gardener's to exercise common sense and think first about the implications of their actions—before they begin ravaging the environment for the sake of a few flowers."

—*The Milwaukee Journal Sentinel*

"Gillman's research can help you save time, money, effort, and the environment."

—*The Monterey County Herald*

"Takes a hard look at some products and practices we consider organic."

—*The South Florida Sun-Sentinel*

"This book plays an important role in debunking the black/white oversimplifications about 'organic' as good and 'synthetic' as bad."

—GardenRant.com

THE Truth ABOUT Organic Gardening

BENEFITS, DRAWBACKS, AND THE BOTTOM LINE

Jeff Gillman

TIMBER PRESS

Portland • London

Published in 2008 by Timber Press, Inc.

The Haseltine Building
133 S.W. Second Avenue, Suite 450
Portland, Oregon 97204-3527
www.timberpress.com

2 The Quadrant
135 Salusbury Road
London NW6 6RJ
www.timberpress.co.uk

Printed in the United States of America

Third printing 2008

Library of Congress Cataloging-in-Publication Data
Gillman, Jeff, 1969–
  The truth about organic gardening : benefits, drawbacks, and the
bottom line / Jeff Gillman.
      p. cm.
  Includes bibliographical references and index.
  ISBN-13: 978-0-88192-862-4
  1. Organic gardening. 2. Agricultural pests—Control. I. Title.
  SB453.5.G54 2008
  635'.0484—dc22
                                           2007022076
A catalog record for this book is also available from the British Library.

Mar 2010

For Clare and Catherine

Contents

Preface

Everyone likes to pick sides. In politics you're either a Republican, a Democrat, or a "stealing votes from people who can actually win" Independent. In sports you're for the team I like or you're against it, and let's not even bother discussing religion, where the consequences of choosing incorrectly are so grave that one may prefer not even to contemplate the possibility of being wrong. Thank goodness that we who inhabit the relaxed world of the garden can find respite and avoid such infernal bickering. No one will ever tell us how to grow our plants. We can do as we please, enjoying experimentations with a new color scheme, a new plant variety, or a different pruning technique, and never hear a nasty word from our neighbors and friends. Yes, it's all quite sublime among those who grow and enjoy plants—that is, until you start to have problems and decide to spray a pesticide or apply a fertilizer. Then everyone seems to want to pass judgment.

Gardeners, both those who grow things for a living and those who grow things for fun, are generally a well-educated group who understand the workings of Mother Nature as well as anyone you can name. And, realizing this, they tend to have strong opinions about how Mother Nature should be treated. Unfortunately, these opinions are not always in tune with those of other gardeners. One group will claim that the only way to grow something properly is to grow it as it would grow naturally, so they provide nothing that they consider unnatural to their plants, forgoing all fertilizers, pesticides, and sometimes even plastic containers. Another group of gardeners will provide things to help their plants grow, but only those things that they construe as natural. Fertilizers are fine as long as they come from a once-living thing, as are pesticides as long as they aren't made in a lab. And finally, another group of gardeners, one much maligned by the other two, will add anything to their plants if they think it will keep them healthy, never mind the source.

It's unfortunate that in a society that's becoming more and more informed by the day, most of the information you'll find on gardening is written by people who reside so firmly in one of these three schools of thought that they're unable to see beyond their biases and into the truth behind the practices they use and recommend. I wrote this book to help the gardener, the weekend farmer, and the educated consumer see beyond dogma and into the truth behind different gardening practices, organic or otherwise.

Acknowledgments

A number of people deserve to be recognized for the help they provided with this book. My family has been very supportive and understanding of my preoccupation with working on it, as have the good people at the University of Minnesota. Chad Giblin deserves credit for brainstorming bits of this book and always providing a critical voice regarding my ideas. A second critical voice was that of Lois Braun, a fair-minded and deep-thinking graduate student who has taught me much more than I could ever teach her. Thanks to Lorraine Anderson for her thorough reading and careful criticism.

1

Organic Basics

When I read books, especially those that deal with issues that might be considered controversial in any way, I find it useful to understand the background of the person who wrote the book. So in the interest of fairness I think it's only appropriate that you understand a little bit about my background and what I believe about growing plants naturally, or "organic" gardening.

I was raised in southeastern Pennsylvania, where my family owned a four-acre orchard that we lived on. (Actually the parcel of land was thirteen acres, but most of this land was rented out to a local farmer who grew hay and corn on it.) We grew peaches, apples, apricots, plums, and pears at various times, and at the times when the orchard was most productive, my father, a research chemist by trade, applied "synthetic" pesticides, such as Sevin and oil, to the trees. Later on, when the kids got older, he stopped spraying so much, preferring to spend his weekends doing things like family travel and working on his motorcycle collection, but that's a different story. In years when he didn't apply chemicals our fruit yields were greatly reduced and I remember digging maggots out of apples with my pocketknife so that I could eat them (the apples—not the maggots). This was such a common occurrence that I remember being quite surprised when some visiting relatives weren't interested in eating these apples that doubled as insect motels. There can be no doubt that living on that small orchard prevented me from becoming a particularly picky eater, but it also led me to believe that to produce fruit, at least fruit that my relatives would eat, you had to apply pesticides.

When I went to graduate school to study entomology and horticulture I was taught both chemical and cultural means of pest control, as most students who study agriculture are, and I quickly found that chemical control provided the more satisfying, albeit short-lived, results, while cultural controls usually worked well over the long term but were rather disappointing in terms of quick results. As a graduate student and research assistant I had the opportunity to participate in projects and experiment with many different pest control methods, from experimental insect trapping to synthetic pesticide use.

When I became a professor and started teaching others about growing plants and controlling pests (at the time that this is written I teach courses in both nursery production and pesticide use), I did a great deal of reading on pesticides to supplement my knowledge so that I would feel more comfortable teaching my subject. One of the areas I focused on was the use of organic and synthetic chemicals, because in my place of employment, the Department of Horticultural Science at the University of Minnesota, we have students from diverse backgrounds. Some of these students are quite experienced in the use of pesticides and some are quite experienced in growing things without pesticides. Needless to say, I expected to be challenged from all sides, and I wanted to be ready with some answers. I wanted to know if pesticides and especially synthetic pesticides were bad, and what I really hoped to find was a conclusive set of studies or maybe a "silverbullet" paper that had all of the answers. Instead what I found was a lot more questions.

In my quest to find out the truth about how toxic pesticides are, I took a few weeks, which eventually turned into months and then years, and spent my spare time looking through scientific articles, both old and new, investigating the dangers of these products. I spent countless hours reviewing toxicity studies that looked at how poisonous various pesticides are to various animals, pesticide modes of action that revealed how pesticides affect their target organisms, and epidemiological studies that followed groups of people who had been exposed to various pesticides over time and tracked their health. And what did I discover from all of this work? The only thing I determined for sure was that many people out there have strong opinions either for or against the use of synthetic pesticides. What I didn't find was enough research to back up conclusively most of the claims of those who oppose or support the use of synthetic pesticides. Instead, I found that every pesticide, indeed every pest control prac-

tice, must be investigated individually and that the broad sweeping conclusions about the whole universe of synthetic pesticides that some organic proponents make are unfounded. I did find that allegations about *particular* pesticides are well founded and that some pesticides are quite dangerous. Not all of these dangerous pesticides are synthetic compounds, though. Researchers often find that organic pesticides have negative effects that are strikingly similar to those of their synthetic counterparts.

Pesticides, however, are only one small part, some would say the smallest part, of organic gardening. So what about the other more important organic practices that have to do with enriching and caring for the soil? Many of these organic practices are good, and many of the standard practices can damage soil, but simply assuming that a practice is good or bad because it is organic or nonorganic is a surefire way to get yourself into all kinds of trouble. Just as with pesticides, any practice we carry out in our gardens to treat our soil needs to be investigated before we use it.

Perhaps at this point you're asking yourself if I've really answered the question posed at the beginning of this introduction, whether I believe organic growing is beneficial. My answer is that I believe that every practice we use in our yards and gardens or with our crops must be assessed individually, in concert with the situation in which we find ourselves and with the other practices we're using. I don't believe that any practice, or any pesticide for that matter, is inherently good or evil, but that we must use these practices and pesticides in wise ways that acknowledge their inherent strengths and weaknesses. People who say that because something is "natural" it's good are oversimplifying just as much as those who say that any old chemical that kills a pest is good.

The goal of this book is neither to promote nor to attack organic gardening. Indeed, I believe that, in general, organic gardening has been a boon to society. However, the term *organic* has been used to promote some practices that while they may be "natural" are not necessarily in the best interest of humans, animals, or nature.

What is organic gardening?

So what does the word *organic* actually mean? When chemists use the term they're referring to the presence of carbon in a particular molecule, but the presence of carbon has nothing to do with whether a compound is considered acceptable for growing a plant organically today. In an upcoming section we'll investigate the origins of the word *organic*, but for now let's say that in the context of growing plants, it would be more appropriate to substitute the word *natural* for the word *organic*, though it's true that it's possible under current regulations to get away with using some synthetic chemicals when growing organically.

The distinction between organic gardening and organic growing must be addressed before we really begin to talk about what it means to garden organically. Organic gardening infers that you're dealing with a small plot of land, maybe only the size of a container, and that you're gardening primarily for yourself rather than for other people. When you're gardening organically you can choose to do almost anything you want to your plants, and though you may disappoint people around you or even yourself, by your choices you won't be breaking any rules or regulations. You have every legal right to apply a pesticide if you determine that choice is the only course of action that will save your tomatoes. Organic growing includes organic gardening but also includes the organic production of food for market. If you're growing things to be sold to other people, you must follow federal regulations in order for the food you produce to be considered organic. This book is written primarily for organic gardeners rather than for people planning to take their produce to market. Indeed, though I hope this book will provide valuable insights for commercial producers, those planning to grow food organically for sale will be better served by acquiring a copy of the USDA regulations that govern the use of organic practices for commercial growers and following these guidelines.

How organic is organic enough?

Some people who grow plants organically take the word *natural* to an extreme and never grow plants using anything that wouldn't have found its way into their gardens naturally if humans had never roamed the earth. In other words, they avoid spraying or fertilizing plant materials with synthetic fertilizers, using plants that aren't from their geographical area, and certainly using transgenic plants. The few additions that these people will consider usually consist of compost, including composted manure, and/or mulch.

Other people who grow plants organically take a more relaxed view of what *natural* means and will spray natural products on their plants though these products may come from halfway around the world and would never have found their way to their current geographical location without the help of humans. These products include everything from neem (a pesticide extracted from a plant grown in South America) to sulfur (an element extracted from mines). Even though you may be able to synthetically produce a chemical that's exactly the same as its naturally occurring counterpart, the synthetic chemical won't be considered organic by this group. Only chemicals that are extracted or gathered from a natural source will be acceptable, with perhaps a few exceptions such as some synthetically produced soaps and oils.

Until relatively recently there was no document that told commercial growers who wanted to use organic production techniques what they could or couldn't do; rather, there were a number of different organizations that would certify growers as organic. These organizations weren't uniform in their approach to organic growing, so there were a variety of practices that one grower could use but that another couldn't because they were certified through different organizations. Then, in 2002, the U.S. Department of Agriculture began implementing a set of National Organic Program Standards that define organic production. These standards aren't set in stone and are subject to reassessment, but now we at least have a uniform understanding across the United States of what *organic* means and what practices we can expect organic producers to use. Although the basics of becoming a certified organic grower are quite straightforward, the list of exact things that you may or may not use is somewhat dynamic, so I would refer you to the USDA's Web page on organic standards (http://www.ams.usda.gov/nop). While these standards are obviously extremely important for commercial growers, to the organic gardener they're little more than a useful set of guidelines; though I'll refer to them as we progress through various garden practices, they have no legal authority regarding what the organic gardener can do in his or her own garden.

Organic gardening is a bit of an enigma in the organic growing world because there are no real regulations that gardeners must follow in order to call themselves organic gardeners; rather, gardeners must decide for themselves whether the practices they use are organic or not. I know people who periodically use synthetic herbicides for weeds but still feel that they're growing plants organically. As long as they understand what they're doing and the probable results of their applications, if it makes them happy and if no one else is affected I really don't have a problem with their actions. The bigger concern is people who decide to garden organically but who don't understand the techniques they use. These people claim they're growing things in a way that benefits themselves and the environment, but their adherence to organics can be problematic in ways they would never suspect.

History of organic growing

Organic growing has been with us since the first people planted seeds and ate what they harvested, but this practice certainly wasn't known as organic growing back then, and it certainly wasn't considered special. Rather, it was considered necessary for survival. So when did the idea of organic growing come about? And how did growing plants using only naturally occurring chemicals get the name *organic*, anyway? I think I can safely say that most people who use organic practices today have little idea about where it all comes from.

One of the first people to use the term *organic* in relation to growing plants was Sir Albert Howard. Howard was without a doubt one of the great researchers of the late nineteenth and early twentieth centuries and also one of the great humanitarians. Though he was from England, Howard lived much of his life in India and served there first as an agricultural advisor and later as the director of the Institute of Plant Industry at Indore. While there he realized that crops over much of the land that the Indians were farming would become less than vigorous over the course of a few years despite the application of fertilizers to the soil. Having an inquisitive mind he researched farming over a large variety of regions, always noting the success that the people of that region had over long stretches of time. The sort of farming he was most in awe of was performed by the people of China. The Chinese have been successfully farming the same regions for centuries without modern technology (though you must remember that modern technology as defined in the early 1900s is quite different from what we define as modern technology today). The key to the success of the Chinese, at least in Howard's mind, was their practice of putting organic (and here I mean carbon-containing) compounds back into the soil that they had just farmed. What type of organic compounds? Well, these compounds varied quite a bit, but primarily manure and compost. Howard was one of the first to fully appreciate nutrient cycling in natural systems in a scientific way and sought to take advantage of these natural processes by using substances that would naturally collect on the soil's surface to fertilize plants and promote crop health. He was keenly aware of the problems associated with unhealthy soils such as increased pressures from diseases and insects and recognized that correcting these problems would go much further in controlling pests than the use of any pesticides. Howard wrote a number of books extolling the virtues of replenishing soils with natural substances, the most important of which is *An Agricultural Testament*, published in 1940.

Sir Albert Howard's work inspired a great number of people, many of whom ended up being more influential than he was. Among the best known of his devotees was Lady Eve Balfour. Balfour was the niece of British Prime Minister Arthur Balfour and a pioneering woman in her own right. She was born in 1899 and was one of the first women to graduate with a degree from the University of Reading. She was motivated and inspired by the works of Howard and actually purchased land with which to test some of his ideas regarding the use of organic matter for stimulating crop growth and health. What she ended up with was the Haughley Experiment, the first side-by-side scientific comparison of organic farming and conventional farming practices (though some might argue about how scientifically rigorous this experiment really was). The results from this experiment were published in her book *The Living Soil* (1943). This work is inspirational to organic growers even today and has done much to promote the use of organic practices.

Despite the influences of Sir Albert and Lady Eve, if I were to select a person who I believe has made the most difference in the promotion of the organic movement, it would without a doubt be Jerome Cohen, a gentleman you might know better as J. I. Rodale (Conford 2001). You're probably familiar with Rodale Press and the Rodale Institute, both named after this early organic icon. Rodale was a pioneer of the early organic movement and with his own publishing house got the organic growing message out better than anybody before or since. Rodale would be considered by some to be quite a fanatic, and if you read some of his earlier writings such as *The Organic Front*, published in 1948, you would see why. Rodale vents and fumes in a way that's both entertaining and compelling, promoting the organic movement and providing ideas and insights for both converted and potential organic growers. Some of his ideas that might seem somewhat off the wall today include the dangers of sulfur (sulfur is an organic standby today) and the health benefits of eating unprocessed apple and orange seeds. Rodale was a pioneer who pushed an agenda focused on the admirable goal of making the world a better place to live. Some of his ideas have become outdated, but some have become commonly accepted. We owe a great debt to Rodale, if not for his specific ideas then at least for his vision of a safer, better world. Rodale was a huge fan of Sir Albert Howard and clearly held Howard in high esteem. Like Howard, Rodale was primarily concerned with the use of organic matter as a soil amendment rather than with pesticides, and though he certainly spoke of pesticides as less than savory, his primary target was usually commercial synthetic fertilizers.

If Rodale was one of the greatest promoters of the organic movement, certainly one of the greatest architects of our modern ideas about what it means to grow plants organically was Rachel Carson, who I feel obliged to say is one of my personal heroes, or in this case, heroines. Today she is considered a pioneer by many, but her writings are also considered a barrier to the use of modern pest control techniques because of the fear of pesticides she helped to instill in our population.

Carson published the book *Silent Spring* in 1962 and through it influenced and encouraged the world to sit up and take notice of the dangers of pesticides. She wasn't a professional researcher or an academic, but she did understand science and was an excellent writer with a clear message and a commitment to making the world a better place. Her book was readable, clear, and believable, and it altered the course of human involvement with pesticides forever by prompting people to encourage our government to take pesticides seriously as a threat to public and environmental health. Carson wasn't primarily concerned with the soil as were Rodale, Balfour, and Howard; rather, she was concerned about the use and overuse of pesticides, primarily insecticides (most notably DDT and its close chemical relatives). Carson's predecessors were certainly opposed to the use of pesticides, but she was the one who spotlighted their dangers in a way that was scientifically based, truthful, and appealing.

Opponents of organic growing have attacked *Silent Spring* repeatedly, pointing out that the studies that Carson looked at were flawed and that her interpretations of their data were not appropriate and, furthermore, that she used scare tactics to achieve her goals. Obviously all of the science that she cited wasn't perfect. The scientific techniques that we use today are far superior to those that were used when she was writing her book, but that doesn't mean that this older work isn't valid. She reached conclusions that were not too terribly unbelievable for the research available at the time. Most important, regardless of specific points, she made people think about what they were doing to their environment.

Over the years a huge number of critics, the first of whom came soon after Howard, have attacked the organic movement. Early detractors, although certainly critical of the whole organic movement, were also relatively thoughtful and fell short of the somewhat more radical critiques sometimes seen today. I think I'm justified in using the word *skeptics* for these people rather than *critics*, which I think is a bit too extreme and better reserved for recent organic movement detractors. If you're interested in finding out why some people don't think organic growing is a good idea, you might look up the works of more recent critics, including *Saving the Planet with Pesticides and Plastics* (1995) by Dennis Avery of the Hudson Institute, and *The Origins of the Organic Agriculture Debate* (2003) by Dr. Thomas DeGregori of the University of Houston. In practice, modern critics of organic production do very little to criticize organic gardening per se; instead they're more concerned with large-scale organic growing and organic foods. Additionally, and more important for the purposes of this book, they defend the use of synthetic fertilizers and pesticides. This defense almost invariably runs contrary to what's written by proponents of organic growing. Although many objective studies have been done on the dangers of pesticides and synthetic fertilizers, the results of these studies often conflict with each other, making a definitive conclusion difficult to reach. In this book I hope to present each practice and chemical in an objective light so that you can reach your own conclusions without the weight of the extreme biases that organic proponents and opponents offer.

2
Understanding Pesticides

The word *pesticide* is a broad term for chemicals intended to kill or repel a wide variety of pests that invade our gardens. A number of different categories of pesticides exist, the most common of which are insecticides, fungicides, and herbicides, meant to control insects, fungi, and plants, respectively. Other lesser-known pesticide categories include rodenticides, meant for rodents; bactericides, meant for bacteria; and avicides, meant for birds.

Much of this book is about ways to control pests and to keep your garden at its best without the use of pesticides. However, because pesticides have been and will continue to be used in gardens and homes, it would be negligent of me not to include mention of them. Many products covered in the next chapters are potentially very dangerous to you and to those around you. Some of these are synthetic, and some are organic. Most of these pesticides are chemicals that can be sprayed, dusted, or otherwise applied to your garden, lawn, or home in some way. Before I start discussing specific chemicals it's worth spending just a few pages on the basics of the chemicals you buy off garden center shelves so that the terms used make sense to you. This information applies to both organic and synthetic chemicals, so don't think that just because you've decided to use only organic sprays you can avoid this section. You can't.

The label

Throughout this book I will harp on the fact that you need to read the label before you use a pesticide. Why? First, because the label is mandated by law and if you don't follow it you're breaking the law. Second, because the label includes information you need in order to apply the chemical effectively and safely. And finally, because the label will provide information about what's actually in the container you've purchased.

Like a food product, every pesticide you purchase will include on the container a list of active ingredients. If you want information about a particular pesticide, the best thing to do isn't to look up the trade name of that product, since trade names change all the time; instead, look up the chemicals listed on the container as active ingredients. This will give you much more information about the specific problems and benefits of the pesticide you're considering. As you work your way through this book you'll see a number of chemicals, both organic and synthetic, listed. Though I mention a few trade names, most of the information I provide is based on the active ingredients in the pesticide, not on the trade names that stare at you from garden center shelves.

Among the greatest concerns people have about pesticides is the toxicity of the pesticide to humans. There's a quick way to tell this: look for one of three signal words front and center on the pesticide label. These words are *Caution*, *Warning*, and *Danger*. The word *Danger* is always accompanied by a skull and crossbones. Pesticides with the word *Caution* are the least toxic (not nontoxic), followed by pesticides with the word *Warning*, and finally pesticides with the word *Danger*. Very few situations that I can think of would warrant selecting a pesticide with the word *Danger* on it. In some cases you'll notice that two products with the same active ingredient have different signal words. These signal words may be different because of the way the active ingredient is delivered; for example, liquid pesticides are often more dangerous than granular pesticides and both of those are usually more dangerous than baits. The difference in signal words could also be because the different products have different concentrations of the active ingredients.

Pesticide delivery

A pesticide can be delivered to its target (the pest you want to get rid of) in all kinds of ways. The most common is as a spray. Some sprays come ready to use, sometimes indicated by the letters *RTU* on the label. Other pesticides need to be mixed. Those that need to be mixed are usually more concentrated, and hence more dangerous, than RTU sprays. Pesticides may also come in a solid form, either as dusts or granules. Dusts and granules are usually somewhat safer than liquids, though there's a chance of inhaling dusts (and granules as well, but to a lesser extent). Inhalation of any pesticide can cause very serious health problems.

Besides liquids and dusts, baits can also be purchased. Baits are usually (but not always) safer than other formulations despite the fact that the bait often includes much more toxic chemicals. This is because the chemicals that baits include often need to be ingested to work and because baits, such as the baits in ant traps, are often covered by a protective shell of cardboard or plastic that makes it difficult for nontarget organisms, like dogs, to get to the poison. When baits aren't encased in a protective shell or trap, they may in some cases be more dangerous to animals in the area because the bait may draw animals to the poison. An example of this is the slug and snail killer metaldehyde, which is often applied as a bait without a protective shell and which may be attractive to some pets, potentially causing major problems.

Environmental impact quotients (EIQs) and toxicological effects

A standardized way to look at pesticides, both organic and synthetic, to determine the differences in their relative dangers to humans and the environment is called the environmental impact quotient (EIQ). This idea was conceived by Joseph Kovach and his colleagues in the early 1990s. EIQs are broken into three parts: risk to the farm worker (basically this means the person who mixes and applies the poison), risk to the consumer of the sprayed product, and risk to the environment. These parts are then averaged, producing a single number that represents the pesticide's potential for damaging the environment and hurting people—or, in other words, the total risk associated with that product. The highest EIQs are likely to be around 100 and the lowest around 10. The higher the number, the greater the chance that the pesticide will negatively impact the environment (including people), and the lower the number, the lower the potential for impact.

EIQs aren't written in stone. They can change over time and will certainly differ somewhat in different situations. The EIQs of various pesticides are updated as additional information becomes available. The numbers that comprise a product's EIQ are calculated by taking farm rather than garden applications into account, so the danger of a pesticide to a gardener may be lower or higher than indicated by the EIQ. Additionally, EIQs are calculated by using a standard concentration of the pesticide so may actually be lower or higher than indicated depending on the concentration at which the pesticide is mixed and applied. Finally, EIQs may differ among products that have the same active ingredients because different inactive ingredients may be present.

Nonetheless, EIQs provide a useful place to start when assessing the potential danger of applying a particular chemical. Though EIQs are not on pesticide labels, they can be found on the Web by typing "environmental impact quotient" into a search engine, or you can try the Web address for Dr. Kovach's work, http://nysipm.cornell.edu/publications/eiq/default. asp. In the following chapters I'll be mentioning the EIQs of a number of pesticides. In most cases where I mention a specific chemical, I'll include its EIQ if that value is available. As new information becomes available EIQs may change. All of the EIQs contained in this book come from an article originally written by Joseph Kovach and his coworkers in 1992 that's updated periodically.

EIQs aren't perfect, but they're the only way I know of to provide a single coherent value that summarizes the potential risk a chemical application poses to both the environment and us. Some pesticides have low EIQs that I think should be higher, and some pesticides have high EIQs that I think should be lower (and in some places in this book I will make my feelings known), but in general my opinion is that EIQs are a useful tool that must be used in concert with the other tools we have at our disposal to help us decide which pesticides are most appropriate for us. Keep in mind that multiple applications of something with a low EIQ may well be worse for the environment than a single application of something with a higher EIQ. I hope, however, that you're applying pesticides infrequently enough that this doesn't become a concern.

As you read about the organic and synthetic pesticides discussed in the coming chapters, you'll notice that I've at times included some information on the toxicological effects of compounds. This information isn't meant to frighten or intimidate you but rather to illustrate the fact that pesticides, both natural and synthetic, have a certain degree of risk associated with them. Risk of this sort can be reduced by reducing the amount of pesticides applied to your garden and lawn, something I strongly endorse.

Later on in this book I describe the risks associated with synthetically and organically grown foods. Before I start discussing specific poisons, I want to point out that poisons are largely dose dependent—in other words, a poison isn't a poison below a certain dose, and likewise a nonpoison may become a poison above a certain dose. This is important to understand, because any pesticide can be incredibly toxic above a certain dose and completely benign below a certain dose. The dose is, of course, governed by the specific pesticide we're talking about. A great example is salt, which when sprinkled lightly on French fries can enhance flavor, but in a dose of only two tablespoons is likely to be toxic to a one-year-old child.

Dose isn't the only factor that governs the effects of a pesticide; frequency also takes a toll. The less frequently a pesticide is used, the less likely it is to negatively affect a person or the environment. All pesticides, organic and synthetic, build up in the environment to one degree or another, though some pesticides break down more rapidly than others. If you have an interest in toxicology, especially as it relates to pesticides, there's no better book than M. Alice Ottoboni's *The Dose Makes the Poison* (1997). I strongly recommend it to anyone who wants to understand how pesticides are tested.

3

Soil Enrichment and Fertilization

Since humans first started eating plants we've been dependent on the quality of the soil in which they grow for our nutrition and health. When people began farming many thousands of years ago they assumed that nothing they could do to the earth would damage it for any period of time, but as they put crops on the same piece of land year after year they slowly but surely found that the earth could be depleted and that ground that once produced beautiful crops could be made to produce almost nothing. The heart of organic gardening and growing is the use of soil in a way that minimizes the damage that constant crop production can wreak on a piece of land. As a gardener you probably put your garden on the same plot of land year after year, just like a farmer does. By treating this area well you can ensure that you will have a healthy place to garden for years to come.

As we get into the nitty-gritty of the practices you can follow to enrich the soil, I first need to recommend one incredibly important step in your gardening process: get a soil test done. Go to your local extension service, get the little bags they use for soil samples, and get that soil tested so that you know how bad or good it is. The information provided with soil tests varies by state, but at the very least you should be able to get information on the texture (sand, clay, loam), quantity of organic matter, acidity (pH), and amount of potassium and phosphorus in your ground. For a little extra money (again, depending on the state) you should also be able to find out the amount of nutrients such as calcium, magnesium, iron, and manganese in your soil and whether the levels are adequate. This information is extremely valuable right before you plant because while you can easily make corrections to your soil before planting, making corrections after planting can be quite difficult.

The information you get when you wisely submit your soil sample to your local extension office will then guide you as you work to make your garden the best it can be. Sandy soils require more fertilization and irrigation than clay soils. Clay soils retain water more effectively and may present a situation where plants are easily overwatered and drowned. By identifying the type of situation you have before you start planting, you'll have a much better understanding of what the soil will do when you prepare it to receive the plants or seed you want to grow.

Though clay and sand make up the major portion of soil, other parts are very important to a soil's health and help to determine how your plants will fare. The best soils usually contain about 3 to 10 percent organic matter. Knowing the amount of organic material in your soil will go a long way toward establishing the amount of work you need to do to get that ground ready to receive plants. Organic matter is nothing more than carbon compounds donated by dead plants and animals (which are composed primarily of carbon). Compost is the most common form of organic matter added to soil, but dead hamsters buried in the backyard will add organic material too, as will anything that was once living.

Organic matter is important because it's so efficient at holding water and nutrients and subsequently releasing them to plants growing in the area. Also, because organic matter was a living entity once, it contains the nutrients that living entities collect over time, hence usually has many nutrients useful to plants in it. Organic matter can drastically improve the structure of the soil and how it affects your plants in a variety of ways. In sandy soils organic matter can provide a network that helps to hold water and nutrients, and in clay soils organic matter can provide pores that increase the amount of air (needed by plant roots) that infiltrates the ground. So as you can see, organic matter is useful regardless of the type of soil you have, and most of the practices for preparing the land that the wise organic grower, and even the conventional grower, uses are focused on increasing the amount of organic material in the soil.

Choices free of synthetic chemicals

Most of the choices for soil preparation involve adding organic matter and physically disrupting weeds and their habitats. Although these practices tend to be labor intensive, they also tend to produce extremely good results, especially in terms of the long-term health of the soil. With all of these practices be sure to keep in mind that other options exist. Often, when reading gardening books, I'm dumbfounded by the lack of options the authors present. Many, many methods can be used to prepare land for plants. The problem isn't identifying these methods, it's figuring out which ones are right for you.

Compost and manure

A primary concern you should have when you start a garden is whether the soil has all of the things it needs. These things consist mainly of nutrients and organic matter but also include appropriate pH, bacteria, and fungi. If the ground you're growing plants in doesn't contain all of the things it needs, you must find a way to supply what's lacking. This usually means applying compost.

Compost comes from once-living creatures and so contains the nutrients needed by plants to grow and maintain their health. Compost is nothing more than organic matter (once-living things) that has been broken down by microorganisms. Because these microorganisms break things down slowly the nutrients in compost are offered to the plant for a long period of time. In our modern society where we like to enjoy things right now, waiting for something to break down isn't seen as a particularly attractive alternative, but that doesn't mean that this type of fertilization is outdated or undesirable. The advantage of this type of fertilization is that it offers not only nutrients but also the organic matter that's the staple of healthy soil.

Manure (and here we're talking about animal waste, not green manure, discussed later) is a great addition to land and is actually quite similar to compost. Fresh manure does have a place in agriculture, but for the average gardener, fresh manure shouldn't be used because it can release ammonia, which can badly injure plants. Rather, manure should be composted before it's used. This composting not only takes care of the ammonia but also serves to kill off many human pathogens that may reside in animal feces. Once manure has been composted it's a valuable amendment for the preparation of land as it offers organic matter as well as a relatively high level of nutrients compared to other composts.

Though fertilizer companies, both those hawking organic and those producing synthetic fertilizers, would have you believe otherwise, most soils are perfectly capable of sustaining plant life unless they've been highly disturbed by humans. What does highly disturbed mean? Well, if your yard was a building only a few years ago, it's highly disturbed. If your yard was once a field used for farming, it's probably highly disturbed.

Compost is the most basic of all of the things you can add to disturbed land to build it up. This substance can be made up of a variety of different things, but in the typical homeowner's garden it's composed of yard and food waste such as grass clippings, leaves, melon rinds, corn husks, coffee grounds, banana peels, and maybe even fish bones. Compost is a type of organic fertilizer, but because the amount of nutrition varies widely from one person's compost pile to another I think it's best to treat compost as an enriching soil amendment rather than as a fertilizer. Do realize, however, that if you're giving your plants a healthy helping of compost, it usually isn't necessary to supply much extra nutrition through a separate fertilizer. What's a healthy dose of compost? About one hundred pounds (or a layer of a third to a half inch deep) per one hundred square feet tilled or otherwise added into the soil every year should be enough, though recommendations vary and anything is better than nothing.

In some localities it's not legal to put food wastes into compost. This is because of the propensity of compost containing food waste to smell bad and attract vermin. If such compost isn't composted long enough before it's used it may also contain human pathogens. Though there are many books out there describing different ways to compost, the best and most up-to-date source of information is your local agricultural extension service.

Organic matter that hasn't been composted is a good addition to gardens in the long run but probably isn't appropriate for most gardens in the short term. Organic matter that hasn't been allowed to compost for long enough—for example, fresh sawdust—has a tendency to hog all of the available nitrogen, leading to malnutrition in the plants you're trying to grow. What happens, in a nutshell, is that the microbes that are breaking down the organic matter suck up the nitrogen for their own uses so the plants can't get to it. After the organic matter is broken down the nitrogen again becomes available. This means that in the short term, plants that are placed in uncomposted organic matter will suffer nutrient deficiencies. One of the places I've seen this happen is in the container production of trees, where an unscrupulous grower will harvest a plant from a field and then put it in a container filled with sawdust. In this situation the plant will look fine for a few months and then will rapidly go downhill as all of the nitrogen in the container is used up by microbes breaking the sawdust down into compost.

Besides the problem of nutrient deficiencies, another potential problem with uncomposted organic matter is that of disease. Using animal excrement as a fertilizer is certainly one of the most controversial organic practices, owing to the fact that animal manure can contain human pathogens. For organic growers who sell their produce this is less of a problem as the government currently requires them to compost their manure in a way that ensures that there's little danger of contamination. For organic gardeners the situation is different because technically there's no control over how long you must compost your manure before you use it. For those of you thinking, Wow! That's great! I don't need to compost! do be aware that *Escherichia coli* (the dreaded *E. coli*) can live in uncomposted manure for twenty-one months (Kudva, Blanch, and Hovde 1998). Believe me, you want to compost manure. How should you compost it? Consult your local agricultural extension for the best methods in your locale, but trust me when I say that the longer you compost manure, the safer your compost will be.

The issue of pathogens in compost is actually more important while maintaining the soil than during preparation because there will be considerable time between soil preparation and the harvesting of crops, whereas there may not be much time between application of natural fertilizers and harvest if you've decided to add these fertilizers later in the season. Any pathogens that cause disease in humans are most likely to be dangerous if the manure is applied right before harvest—as it might be for a crop like apples, which ripen in the fall at about the same time that growers like to apply natural fertilizer.

BENEFITS Compost is a wonderful addition to soils, offering nutrients and improving water retention and drainage. It's also a great way to use what might otherwise be considered garbage.

DRAWBACKS Adding organic matter to areas that are already full of organic matter (like bogs) is usually not necessary. Uncomposted organic matter sucks up nitrogen and may contain harmful micro-organisms. Manures, if they aren't properly treated, may well contain levels of human pathogens that are unacceptable.

THE BOTTOM LINE The practice of adding compost, including composted manure, to soil is a good one as long as you compost appropriately.

Natural fertilizers

Natural fertilizers such as bonemeal, blood meal, seaweed extracts, alfalfa meal, fish emulsions, and composted manure have been in use for as long as people have had gardens. These fertilizers offer a wide range of nutrients beyond the simple nitrogen, phosphorous, and potassium that many of the synthetic fertilizers do, but they tend to offer their nutrients at a low concentration because of the source from whence they come (dead plants and animals). Also, their nutrition tends to be available to plants slowly instead of rapidly as with many synthetic fertilizers because of the low solubility of most of these products.

The slower release of nutrients from many of the natural fertilizers makes them a better choice for applying when preparing the land than most synthetic fertilizers are. For example, one application of composted manure, about a half pound per square foot of garden area tilled into the soil, is usually all a vegetable garden or flower bed needs in a year. By contrast, synthetic fertilizers that aren't specifically labeled as slow release will need to be reapplied two or three times to a typical vegetable garden or flower bed because they move through the ground quickly and are available to the plant for only a relatively short period of time.

BENEFITS Natural fertilizers supply nutrients over a much longer period of time than most synthetic fertilizers, are less likely to burn plants than synthetic fertilizers, and contain micronutrients that synthetic fertilizers may not.

DRAWBACKS Because natural fertilizers don't release a lot of nutrients all at once, you don't get the thrill of seeing your plants turn from a dull green to a lustrous, almost sickeningly bright green in the span of a few days like you can with synthetic fertilizers. It's possible to overfertilize with natural fertilizers, just like synthetic ones.

THE BOTTOM LINE Natural fertilizers are a great source of nutrients for your garden. You rarely need to apply these fertilizers more than once a year because of their slow release. If you're using compost you probably don't need to use them at all.

Green manure and cover crops

The word *manure* is used by most as a polite way to say poop. Among farmers, especially in the early part of the twentieth century and prior, the word *manure* was actually used to indicate anything that can supply nutrients to the soil. In fact, synthetic fertilizers were referred to by Sir Albert Howard as "artificial manures." Poop is certainly a substance that can deliver nutrients, but it's far from the only one. Plants that are grown in an area and then cut down and allowed to rot will supply nutrients to future crops, because as a crop rots it gives off the nutrients that it stored while it was growing. These plants are known as "green manure." A related but somewhat different term important to the organic gardener is *cover crop*. All green manures are considered cover crops, but not all cover crops are green manures. Cover crops are any plants grown on a piece of land when the usual crops are not there, regardless of whether the plants find their way back into the soil. A green manure crop is a type of cover crop that necessarily finds its way back into the soil where it was grown after it dies, ensuring that the nutrients that it collected during its life will find their way back into the soil.

If you've ever been a farmer or had the opportunity to work on a farm, you've probably heard of farmland becoming "cropped out." This slang term means that the land has been used up and can no longer support satisfactory crops. What does that mean practically? It means that the land has lost a great deal of nutrition and organic matter through crop harvest and erosion.

When crops are harvested, all of the good things that were in the soil and that the plant took up during its life leave the land. Over time this can create problems if the nutrients that are taken aren't properly replenished.

Synthetic fertilizers, which are basically nothing more than salts, can certainly help to put nutrition back into the soil; however, these fertilizers are usually high in nitrogen, phosphorus, and potassium and somewhat lacking in other nutrients required for plant life. Additionally, synthetic fertilizers, especially those used in agriculture, are often very soluble, which results in their relatively rapid exit from the land, either by leaching into the land or by running off of it. Green manures will last in an area much longer than most synthetic fertilizers; they will offer not only nutrients but also organic matter that will help to retain the nutrients that are applied, including those that come from synthetic fertilizers.

Using green manures to prepare for future crop plantings is a common practice in many production scenarios, such as when trees are grown in a field for harvest. In this situation a great deal of soil leaves the production facility when the trees are harvested. To replenish the land by cycling organic matter and nutrients back into the soil, green manures are often planted for one to three years.

Some common green manure crops include various fast-growing grasses such as sudan grass, corn, and even plants that we might normally think of as weeds such as clover. The advantage of clover and similar plants, called legumes, is that these plants actually take nitrogen right out of the air and after they die or are killed, deliver this nitrogen to the crops grown next, hence decreasing the need for addition of nitrogen-containing fertilizers.

Crops used as green manures are chosen by farmers and gardeners for a variety of reasons, most commonly their cost and their difference from the plants usually grown for money or for show. It's almost always preferable to plant something besides the "money" crop or related species as green manure because if pathogens infest the green manure crop and that crop is similar to the "money" crop, the disease could stay in the soil and cause future problems.

BENEFITS After green manure crops are cut down they provide nutrients and organic matter for your regular crops. Both green manure and cover crops help to hold the soil and prevent erosion.

 DRAWBACKS The biggest problem with green manure crops is that the land isn't available for any other use while these crops are growing.

Management can be somewhat time sensitive as it's important to cut these crops down before they produce seeds; otherwise the cover crop may become a weed of your regular crops.

THE BOTTOM LINE Using green manures is certainly a beneficial practice. If you farm, green manures are all but necessary to ensure continued production from your fields. If you're a homeowner, you're probably dealing with a relatively small parcel of land and may not want to have your limited space filled up with tall grasses or clover for too long. If this is the case, you might be better off adding other sources of organic material such as compost to your land instead of green manures.

Intercrops

An attractive way to maintain land is by using a practice called intercropping. Intercropping involves planting two or more different types of plants in the same location. Often intercropping is used for insect and disease control and we'll take a look at using it for those purposes in later chapters, but to me the most interesting use of intercrops is as a way to increase the amount of organic matter in your garden. Like green manures, intercropping to increase organic matter involves planting a second crop intended to be cut and left where it falls. Unlike green manures, intercrops are planted right alongside the regular crop.

One common use of intercrops is in the production of trees. In this situation rows of trees are planted normally and the area immediately around the trees is kept free of grass and weeds through the use of herbicides to reduce competition for nutrition and water, but grass is grown in between the trees and is cut multiple times during the year. The grass holds the ground and reduces the amount of erosion that occurs with rains, and every mowing adds more organic material to the ground.

The easiest, and often the best, intercrops are tall grasses that grow quickly and can be cut down before they produce seeds. Other options that can work well include red clover, beans, and other legumes that take nitrogen from the air and when they're cut down or killed with an herbicide actually provide some fertility to your crops. Do remember that it's necessary to cut down intercrops before they seed in order to get the greatest benefit and have the least hassle from them.

BENEFITS Intercrops allow a gardener to build high levels of organic matter in a garden without skipping a year with the regular plants. If legumes are used, some nitrogen is added to the soil when these plants are cut down (but not before). Other benefits of intercropping are pointed out in the chapters on insect and disease control.

DRAWBACKS Intercrops do compete with your regular crops even if you clear the area immediately surrounding the crops. Additionally, intercrops take up space that you might like to use for something else.

THE BOTTOM LINE For large areas of really lousy soil, intercrops are a good idea because they allow you to build up organic matter while still maintaining a crop, unlike cover crops. Unfortunately the loss of space for crops and the competition between the intercrops and the crops you're trying to grow usually mean that this process isn't used as much as it could be.

"Organic" amendments for pH adjustment

Among the most common problems gardeners run into after their plants are in the soil is a nutrient deficiency from a lack of either a specific nutrient or, more commonly, an appropriate pH. Most plants can take up nutrients best at a soil pH of 5.5–6.5, though some plants, such as azaleas and blueberries, do better at a lower pH and some, such as honey locust and bur oak, prefer a higher one. By testing your soil before you plant, you'll be able to predict what nutrients might be lacking because of pH. Armed with this information, you can apply the appropriate amendments to your soil for plant growth.

If you find that your soil isn't in a pH range that's healthy for your plants, you'll need to add amendments to correct that pH. Most of the amendments used for correcting soil pH are considered organic. If the pH is too high (alkaline), sulfur can be used to reduce it; if the pH is too low (acidic), lime can be used to raise it. To determine exactly how much of a product to use, either follow the instructions on the container or, even better, contact your local agricultural extension office for guidance. The people at local extension offices have usually seen soils similar to yours and should be able to provide the best options for your soil.

Adjusting pH by applying lime, sulfur, or something similar can make your soil hospitable to the plants you want to grow.

These amendments are finicky, and broad statements about how much of them to add to get a certain result can be off the mark because soil types, amounts of organic matter, and the like can differ. Amendments that change the natural pH of a soil last for a limited amount of time, perhaps only a year or two, and so need to be reapplied.

The best plants for your yard are those that can handle the natural soil conditions, but if you've just got to have that acid-loving azalea, or if your soil is just naturally way too acidic or alkaline, an amendment may be necessary. If you do use an amendment, be sure to get recommendations from your local agricultural extension office on how much to use.

Choices that include synthetic chemicals

A number of synthetically produced chemicals exist that can aid the growth and health of plants and help to get rid of weeds as you prepare your land. These chemicals are much maligned simply because they're synthetic. My personal feeling is that you should look at each of them separately before you cast a stone at the whole group.

Synthetic fertilizers

Much debate has occurred over the last century regarding the addition of synthetic fertilizers to land. The foundation for many of the criticisms is the propensity farmers used to have for substituting these fertilizers for adding organic matter. Organic matter is such an effective medium for holding nutrients and water, however, that its gradual reduction over the years in fields where farmers relied solely on synthetic fertilizers was extremely detrimental to crops. Nowadays few farmers rely on synthetic fertilizers alone. Current recommendations for soils almost always include the caveat that organic matter must be maintained to produce the best plants possible.

Synthetic fertilizers unquestionably contain nutrients, but they add these nutrients to a site that may not have had to deal with such a high level of nutrition previously. This nutrition can have a harmful effect if it leaches or runs off the site into a waterway, where it can encourage eutrophication. Eutrophication is the enrichment of a body of water with a nutrient such that algae and other organisms grow out of control and effectively reduce the ability of higher life, such as fish, to live in the area. Additionally, the nutrients in the fertilizer had to come from somewhere, and that somewhere for synthetic fertilizers is usually not an easily renewable resource but rather is often a strip mine, which certainly isn't a positive thing for our environment.

The synthetic fertilizers we use on our lawns and gardens are generally salts. When these salts dissolve in water they make their nutrients available to plants. Organic fertilizers are usually a little bit different in that their nutrients are often connected to organic compounds. When these organic compounds break down the nutrients become available. Assertions have been made by organic growers over the years that because organic fertilizers have nutrients that are tied to organic compounds they're better, but that isn't really the case. The nutrients that come from organic and synthetic fertilizers are the same once the plant being fed takes them up into its vascular system; however, organic fertilizers do have the advantage of being available to the plant for a longer period of time than synthetic fertilizers because they take longer to break down. Both organic and synthetic fertilizers can affect soil pH in a positive (or negative) way and provide micronutrients to plants.

Though synthetic fertilizers certainly have their drawbacks, they have some noteworthy benefits as well; otherwise nobody would use them. Synthetic fertilizers deliver nutrition to plants in a way that's quick and sure, they're cheap, they can be formulated to release nutrients slowly, and they can be concentrated so that much less has to be applied to get the same amount of nutrition as an organic fertilizer. Synthetic fertilizers also have the advantage of being produced with a variety of different levels of nutrients. The best of the synthetic fertilizers are probably those that are referred to as slow release, which includes fertilizers encased in a coating that allows the nutrients to be released slowly. These fertilizers are extremely useful for plants growing in containers.

Some contend that synthetic fertilizers disrupt natural ecosystems by overloading them with nutrients. While this outcome doesn't necessarily have to occur, it certainly can. One of the most easily seen effects of synthetic fertilizers is on mycorrhizae, the symbiotic associations of fungi with plant roots. Under natural growing conditions, fungi inhabit the roots of many plants and help the plants to seek out additional nutrition. Under conditions of heavy fertilization, most commonly stemming from synthetic fertilizer use, the growth of these fungi is inhibited. Likewise, the amount and type of other bacteria and fungi in soils is also affected by the amount of nutrition present, and changes affect the natural balance. Whether you're concerned about affecting this natural balance is up to you, but when I use synthetic fertilizers I like to use them very conservatively so as to minimize my effect on natural systems.

Although synthetic fertilizers are made through chemical processes, they aren't exactly the foreign substances that those promoting organic fertilizers would have you believe. Most of the synthetic fertilizers we use are actually quite natural; they've just been treated in a way that some may consider unnatural. (There's a common misconception that synthetic fertilizers include petrochemicals, but that's rarely the case.) This treatment leads some people to avoid them, perhaps deservedly so, but before you decide that synthetic fertilizers are bad it makes sense to understand a little bit more about them and where they come from.

The elements present in most synthetic fertilizers include nitrogen, phosphorus, and potassium. All of these elements are necessary for plant growth and health, but the most important one for growing plants is nitrogen. The reason is that plants are more commonly limited in their growth by the amount of nitrogen available than by the availability of any other elements; if more nitrogen is added, more growth will usually be realized.

Nitrogen fertilizers are the first ones that come to mind when discussing synthetic fertilizers, probably because of the amount of nitrogen added to lawns, gardens, and farms every year. In the 1800s, before synthetic nitrogen fertilizers were available, farmers added some nitrogen to the soil by applying cow manure, horse manure, and other manures. But because these fertilizers had a relatively low concentration of nitrogen, other sources were desired. The fertilizers of choice to increase nitrogen levels were Peruvian guano and Chilean nitrates. Peruvian guano comes from arid regions in Peru and is composed of aged, dried feces from seabirds. Since the seabirds eat large quantities of meat in the form of crabs and other shellfish their guano is very high in nitrogen. Unfortunately, Peruvian guano is a limited resource dependent upon lots of feces and plenty of time, and so this source of nitrogen was quickly used up and became too expensive. Likewise, Chilean nitrates came from mines and were used up so quickly that they soon became too expensive.

In the early 1900s the need for cheap and abundant nitrogen fertilizers among farmers was becoming more and more evident, as was the need for nitrogen in another industry—the military (many common explosives use nitrogen). Chemists turned to the air for answers. The air we breathe is composed of about 70 percent nitrogen, but this nitrogen is only available as N_2. This form of nitrogen works fine to nourish legumes, a group of plants that can take their nitrogen directly from the air, and for some microorganisms, but most plants (and explosives) need a different form of nitrogen to really get their growth going. In fact, even legumes grow faster if they're offered nitrogen as a fertilizer. N_2 isn't easily converted into a form that's available to plants, and so chemists had their challenge before them—find a way to convert this form of nitrogen into one that could be used by plants and for explosives.

The chemists who finally succeeded in harnessing nitrogen from the air were Fritz Haber and Carl Bosch, both of whom received Nobel prizes. Basically they fed nitrogen and hydrogen through a high-temperature, high-pressure chamber in the presence of various metals (most commonly iron ores) to make ammonia (a gas that contains nitrogen; ammonia from the store is actually this gas dissolved in water). Ammonia could then be used to make various other fertilizers. This method of making ammonia is now known as the Haber-Bosch process.

The beauty of the Haber-Bosch process is that the nitrogen that's converted into ammonia comes from a source that's easily replenished by natural processes. Though it wouldn't be appropriate to call this nitrogen-fixing process renewable because of the electric power, usually from the burning of coal, required to create the high temperatures and pressures needed, and because the hydrogen in the reaction usually comes from natural gas, this process does have the virtue of not requiring the mining that the collection of other elements common in fertilizers, such as phosphorus, does.

Over the years proponents of organic growing have made the argument that fertilizer elements, especially nitrogen, should come from natural sources such as leguminous crops. But based on what we know about how much nitrogen can be fixed per acre naturally and how much is needed to grow crops optimally, it's unrealistic to think that all of the world's nitrogen needs could be met by nitrogen from manure and legumes (Smil 2001). Still, this isn't to say that all of the nitrogen in your garden couldn't come from these sources.

Phosphorus used in fertilizers, unlike nitrogen, practically all comes from phosphorus rock, which is mined in various places including Florida and North Carolina. This phosphorus rock is then reacted with other chemicals to make fertilizers such as diammonium and monoammonium phosphate. Did you notice the word *ammonium* in that last sentence? The ammonium used for these chemical processes actually comes from the Haber-Bosch process. Rock phosphate, an organic fertilizer that contains phosphorus, comes from mines in the southern United States; although this fertilizer is organic, the process of acquiring it from the earth is quite detrimental to the area that's mined. Rock phosphate itself isn't a great fertilizer because it takes such a long time for the phosphorus in it to become available to plants.

Potassium fertilizers in the United States come mostly from mining in New Mexico, Utah, California, and Michigan, as well as Saskatchewan. This potassium comes in the form of various salts that collected after the drying up of ancient oceans. This potassium may or may not then be reacted with other chemicals to make different types of potassium fertilizers.

All of this is very interesting (at least to me), but what does it mean to you and your garden? First of all, although what we call synthetic fertilizers often come from chemical processes, the elements themselves are from natural sources. Certainly the air is natural, as is phosphorus rock and the remains of ancient oceans. Does that mean that synthetic fertilizers are good? Well, yes and no. For nitrogen in particular, it takes a significant amount of energy to make that chemical reaction run, and if that energy comes from burning fossil fuels, it depletes our natural resources and may very well contribute to global warming. Potassium and phosphorus need to be mined, which can have quite a negative impact on the earth. In the end I come down on the side of nonmined organic fertilizers for these reasons, and because of their slow release properties, not because they're "natural."

One of the supposed drawbacks of using synthetic fertilizers is that these fertilizers may be harmful to organisms, such as worms and bacteria, living in the ground. Indeed, these organisms don't care for synthetic fertilizers when they're first applied. However, after they've been applied and used by soil-dwelling organisms, the amount of organic material in the ground will increase and so the soil microorganisms and earthworms will actually do better in the long run, as long as synthetic fertilizers aren't continually reapplied.

BENEFITS Synthetic fertilizers offer a rapid and convenient way to get nutrients to your plants. Synthetic slow-release fertilizers are available that can release nutrients more slowly into the soil.

DRAWBACKS The elements of synthetic fertilizers may come from mines that are destructive to the earth. The creation of synthetic nitrogen fertilizers uses a great deal of energy, which may be considered wasteful. Constant reapplication of synthetic fertilizers could change the natural balance of soil organisms.

THE BOTTOM LINE I like organic fertilizers for a number of reasons, the most important of which, at least to me, is that they reuse nutrients from other living sources and so avoid waste. However, I use synthetic fertilizers for certain applications because they're cheap, readily available, and very effective.

Synthetic amendments for nutrition and pH adjustments

A number of synthetic amendments are available that you can use to add fertility to your soil. These amendments usually come from a chemical reaction between the very compounds that we encountered in the earlier section on organic amendments and another chemical, such as sulfuric acid, which is produced basically by heating sulfur with water. Many of these synthetic compounds are acceptable following current USDA organic standards despite the fact that they are synthetically produced. Some of the synthetic amendments that may currently be used by organic growers include iron sulfate, aluminum sulfate, magnesium sulfate, and soluble boron products.

The processes used to make these chemicals are very simple and don't include petrochemicals. These fertilizers and amendments for altering pH are effective, although often they don't last as long as their organic counterparts. For example, iron sulfate moves through the soil much more quickly than sulfur, which means that iron sulfate changes the pH of the ground faster but is effective for a shorter period of time.

 Synthetic pH-changing and nutritional amendments are usually available to a plant faster than their organic counterparts.

 These amendments often don't last in the ground as long as their synthetic counterparts.

 In most situations I prefer the organic choices for nutrient additions and pH alterations, but that doesn't mean that synthetic amendments aren't a good idea when a pH needs to be altered quickly.

THE BEST CHOICES FOR YOU

Should you fertilize your land using organic or synthetic methods? It's a tough choice. For initially enriching the soil before you plant, organic practices make a world of sense. Let me be blunt: I believe strongly in the use of green manure crops and compost to increase the fertility and usefulness of soil. I just don't see any reason not to prepare land by incorporating some sort of organic material into it. These methods will get plants up and going, and although many people like to add other fertilizers to ground that's already received a heavy dose of compost, the truth is that only rarely do you need to add this extra fertilizer.

Keeping fertility at a good level in your garden while you're growing your crops isn't difficult. If you've applied good compost, manure, or some other organic fertilizer, your soil has got what it takes and probably won't need any other nutrition. If you end up not being able to find enough of these organic sources of nutrition for your garden, synthetic sources are certainly acceptable to your plants and they're also cheap. If you do use synthetics, why not also consider growing an intercrop if you have enough space? The intercrop will collect the extra nutrients that your crop doesn't use and return them to your land, as well as increasing the amount of organic material in your soil when it's cut down. In a short time you may not need synthetics at all.

4

Weed Control

Besides enhancing the quality of their soil, the primary concern gardeners have when preparing and maintaining their land is weed control, which is probably the reason herbicides are the most commonly used pesticides across the world. Weeds inhibit the growth of crops by taking up water, nutrients, and even sunlight that we would prefer to see used by the plants we planted.

The easiest thing to do to keep your plot of land weed-free is to periodically cover it with chemicals that inhibit the growth of weeds. The herbicides we use for this include both preemergence herbicides (which affect plants before they break the surface of the soil) and postemergence herbicides (to kill plants that have already emerged from the soil). A number of both of these types of products are available that will do the job. Unfortunately, the increased ease of maintenance that these chemicals offer is balanced by the fact that they may have some toxic effects and might in some cases actually inhibit the growth of crops. In this chapter we'll look at organic and synthetic practices to control weeds, including some that use herbicides and some that don't.

Choices free of synthetic chemicals

All sorts of handy ways exist to get rid of weeds without using synthetic chemicals; some of them are very effective and some of them aren't. My favorites are those that don't include herbicides. Although it's true that a bunch of pretty good organic herbicides are available, few are really outstanding. As a group, organic herbicides tend to be relatively safe (as long as they're used properly, of course!); in fact, as you look through the list, you'll see many that are related to food products in one way or another.

Corn gluten meal

The best, and really only, preemergence product available to those who want to go organic is corn gluten meal. This is a by-product of the corn processing industry that was patented in the early 1990s by a group led by Nick Christians of Iowa State University. Although this preemergence herbicide can be extremely effective at controlling weeds before they emerge, it usually needs to be reapplied for a couple of years to be really effective, and most people find that they can control weeds better and more cheaply by using synthetic chemicals.

About twenty pounds of corn gluten meal is usually recommended for a thousand-square-foot area (that's the area of a piece of land twenty feet by fifty feet). This is a lot—certainly a lot more than you would apply if you were using synthetic chemicals. Fortunately, however, because you have to apply so much it ends up providing about the concentration of nitrogen you'll need in a year in order to maintain a low-input lawn or a healthy garden, which is a really nice plus. Corn gluten meal is very safe; in fact, it's found in cat food. (That doesn't mean you can eat it. It's not for human or animal consumption in the form that you buy it in for pest control.)

BENEFITS Corn gluten meal is an effective preemergence herbicide that will only be useful if you give it a chance to work over a couple of years. It will also provide nutrients to your ground, so if you use it at the recommended concentration (usually about twenty pounds per thousand square feet) you may not need to fertilize.

DRAWBACKS I heard Nick Christians speak a few years ago about his discovery of the herbicidal properties of corn gluten meal. I found it interesting, though not really surprising, that he prefaced his talk by saying that synthetic chemicals could offer better weed control more cheaply than corn gluten meal.

THE BOTTOM LINE This is a useful product that's effective at what it's supposed to do. Though I'm not overly worried by the dangers of most of the synthetic turf herbicides we use, I'm much less worried by the dangers of corn gluten meal. Indeed, this product is used in cat food. Though you must wait, sometimes years, for this product to work, it's an effective preemergence organic herbicide.

Flaming weeds

At your local farm store you can buy a nozzle to hook onto a propane tank that will allow you to spray flames all around your garden to control weeds. Using flames to get rid of weeds isn't a new idea, but it's a good one. A study conducted by Carlene Chase, Johannes Scholberg, and Gregory MacDonald from the University of Florida (2004) showed that flaming was more effective at controlling weeds, especially weeds with better-developed root systems, than organic herbicides based on such things as citric acid, garlic oil, and clove oil, and that the control actually lasted longer than these other treatments too. Flaming offered almost 100 percent control of weeds when weed control was assessed four days after treatment and offered around 80 percent control as much as twenty-one days after treatment. At the nursery I'm in charge of at the University of Minnesota we've used flaming to clear areas of weeds, and while these flames have been reasonably effective, they haven't been as effective as synthetic herbicides.

BENEFITS Flames are more effective than organic postemergence herbicides in most cases.

DRAWBACKS Fire is dangerous, especially on a dry day. A great deal of care needs to be taken when using this method of weed control. You need to be careful of hitting any plant you value. Some weeds will come back from their roots. This method of weed control is not as effective as synthetic herbicides and it takes a little more time to flame an area than simply to apply a spray.

THE BOTTOM LINE This is a good organic method of controlling weeds after they emerge if you're very careful and if you're comfortable with a few weeds surviving.

Garlic oil and clove oil

The other day I was reading through a catalog from a brand new company that advertised an herbicidal spray composed of clove oil and vinegar. This spray is supposed to kill plants by burning them right down to their roots. My reply: So what? You can spray regular old vinegar from your pantry onto plants and burn them down to their roots. If you can show me how to kill those roots, well then you've done something. Garlic oil and clove oil are frequent ingredients in organic sprays and are usually found in conjunction with vinegar. They do a good job of knocking out the shoots of plants, but they're just not that great at knocking out the roots of plants. What that ends up meaning is that repeated applications of herbicides containing these compounds need to be made in order to completely control weeds that are well established. For example, clover, creeping Charlie, and dandelions will turn brown quickly with an application of a clove or garlic oil herbicide, but they'll come right back in most cases because these weeds have such large and strong root systems. The herbicidal spray I began this paragraph with is actually recommended as a control for poison ivy. All I can say is that it has no place in my yard. The leaves of the poison ivy will burn right off, making the plant seem dead, and then it will come right back from the roots.

BENEFITS These oils can certainly kill young plants, and even older plants, if they're continually reapplied. Additionally, these oils, though they shouldn't be considered safe to humans and animals at the concentrations at which they're applied to plants, are certainly less toxic than many other herbicides.

DRAWBACKS These oils won't kill the roots of well-established plants and aren't selective.

THE BOTTOM LINE If you pay close attention to your garden and are willing to go out every week or two to weed, you're dealing with young weeds, and herbicides based on these oils will work fine. Of course, so will hand weeding, and with hand weeding you're less likely to damage your crops through carelessness.

Hand weeding

Get yourself a nice pair of gloves and a good kneeling pad and take the time to get some exercise while excising weeds. This method isn't pretty and it isn't fancy, but if you've got a small garden and just a little bit of time once a week, there's no better way to get rid of weeds, period. If this is the first time you've thought of hand weeding, I've got a few suggestions. Grab the plant you're trying to remove very close to the ground; this will allow you to pull out more of the weed's roots. If you don't manage to pull out most of a weed's roots, there's a good chance the plant will grow back. To get deeper into the soil and remove more of the root system, you might purchase any of a number of gardening tools, usually shaped something like a fork. If you're good at getting out there and weeding regularly, once a week or so, you're in an especially enviable situation, because chances are your weeds will never develop those long root systems that are so hard to pull out.

BENEFITS Exercise, feeling the dirt between your fingers, getting a closer look at your plants to see if anything else is amiss—hand weeding is great for all of these reasons. But for me the beauty of hand weeding is the chance to thoroughly annihilate, in a very personal way, those evil plants that thought they could park themselves right next to my carrots.

DRAWBACKS It requires time. Depending on the size of your garden, it may take a while to thoroughly hand weed.

 THE BOTTOM LINE Even if you don't have much time, hand weeding is still the way to go, if not when you're preparing the land then at least when you switch to maintenance. For most gardens all you need is about an hour a week, and if you can find that hour each and every week, you'll control the majority of your weeds. The work you put in will make your vegetables taste sweeter and your flowers more vibrant—no lie.

Homemade concoctions

Gardeners will try a number of homemade herbicides. These are mostly things like vinegar and mixtures of salt and vinegar but also include concoctions like ground-up brussels sprouts and borax. Vinegar mixtures work similarly to commercial vinegar herbicides though potentially with slightly less effect, because the amount of acetic acid in your vinegar may be a bit lower than in a commercial product. If you do want to use vinegar as an herbicide, it's best to use undiluted vinegar that has 5 percent or more acetic acid. Brussels sprouts don't tend to be very effective at controlling weeds (Gillman 2006). But one cure that doesn't fare too badly, according to some sources, is borax. Research conducted at Iowa State University has shown that borax can control ground ivy (aka creeping Charlie) quite successfully when applied to this weed in Kentucky blue turfgrass (Hatterman-Valenti, Owen, and Christians 1996). Unfortunately, controlling the ground ivy may also result in damage to your turf. The reason the borax works is that it contains boron, which is needed by plants in small quantities but toxic to plants in heavy doses. Weeds such as ground ivy tend to be more susceptible to overfertilization with this element than grasses, so the boron should kill these weeds while leaving grass alone. Though this research from Iowa looks promising, other research from the University of Wisconsin testing a similar mix of borax showed only marginal results (Stier 1999). If you want to try it, the recipe for enough borax spray to cover a thousand square feet is ten ounces of Twenty Mule Team borax dissolved in four ounces of warm water that's then mixed with two and a half gallons of water (Jauron 1997). Be aware that if there's already a high concentration of boron in your soil, you might be making your soil toxic to grass and other desirable plants.

BENEFITS   Homemade concoctions based on vinegar or salt affect weeds quickly. Using borax has the advantage of using a natural element to control weeds.

DRAWBACKS   Homemade vinegar sprays won't kill the roots of weeds, and homemade salt sprays may harm the usual soil ecosystem and future crops. The borax spray may harm your turf or other plants by providing too much boron.

THE BOTTOM LINE   I tend to stay away from homemade sprays. Sure, they all have their good points, but their bad points overpower their benefits for me. Naturally, you have your own priorities and may want to try them out for yourself. If so, I say go for it, but be very careful and understand the possible problems that these remedies can cause.

Mulch

Without a doubt the best method of weed control you can use is mulch. The advantage of mulch is that it not only prevents weeds from growing now but also, if organic, helps to revitalize your soil as it's broken down by soil-dwelling organisms.

Mulch can be either organic or not. Mulch that wouldn't be considered organic by most includes plastic sheets and rubber mulch such as ground-up tires. These types of mulch tend to be extremely effective at blocking out weeds, but they don't break down readily, meaning that they won't provide any nutrition for your plants at a later time. Because these artificial mulches are waterproof, they may block water from reaching the ground where it can do some good for your plants. If mulch is black and pushed up against the stem of a plant it can also lead to heat buildup on the stem, which may cause some stem damage. Gravel is certainly a natural substance, but it has many of the same properties as artificial mulches. It won't break down and so doesn't provide any nutrition, but it also doesn't need to be replaced. Gravel isn't usually as effective at controlling weeds as artificial mulch is, but it doesn't create an impenetrable barrier that water can't go through either.

Mulch that's organic is usually a better choice for gardens because of its propensity to break down and provide nutrition to plants. The many types of organic mulch available include wood chips, pine bark and nuggets, straw, grass clippings, and coffee grounds. You must choose the covering that's best for you. Wood chips have gotten a bit of a bad rap because as some researchers have pointed out, they may take up nitrogen that's intended for trees and they may harbor fungi that could be toxic or that are unsightly and might stain if they're near a house. Certainly all of these considerations are important, but the one that concerns me the most is nitrogen depletion. Wood mulch is full of complex sugars such as cellulose. Microbes like to break these sugars down (basically they eat them) but in order to do that, they need to use nitrogen. Where do they get the nitrogen from? Why, from the earth, of course. Wood chips used around annuals, small perennials, or newly planted trees could well result in a little bit of nitrogen deficiency for your plants. This deficiency should wear off after a short time. Wood mulch that's been slightly composted will suck less nitrogen from the soil. Pine bark and nuggets also tend to draw less nitrogen from the soil, leaving more for your plants.

Incorrect use of mulch can also cause some problems. For example, mulch that's placed right up against the stem of a plant may encourage disease and decay. If the plant is a tree, this can also result in roots growing up into the mulch and then surrounding the trunk of the tree and strangling it to death, a form of tree suicide that most of us would like to avoid. Mulch that's spread too deep will actually raise the water table around the area it covers, potentially reducing the amount of air that gets into the soil and causing plant roots to suffocate, though this usually isn't a major problem except in extreme circumstances. The proper depth for mulch is about two to four inches.

BENEFITS Mulch will help control weeds, maintain a healthy water balance in the soil (unless it's overused), and if organic, provide some fertility over time.

DRAWBACKS Organic mulches such as wood chips are likely to tie up nitrogen for a short time after they're applied. These mulches will also eventually break down, which while providing some nutrition for the tree will also provide a nice environment for weeds to grow in. Finally, if used incorrectly, mulches can lead to overheating of plant stems, can harbor pests including insects and disease, can raise the water table and thus suffocate plant roots, and can even result in stem-girdling roots.

THE BOTTOM LINE Mulches are good, but they need to be used wisely to avoid potential pitfalls.

Pelargonic acid

Pelargonic acid is a naturally occurring compound found in many soaps. It works as an herbicide by causing the cells of plants to break apart; fortunately, it doesn't have the same effect on animal cells. Pelargonic acid has been used quite effectively as a broad-spectrum postemergence herbicide to kill many types of plants. The primary benefit that any gardener will appreciate with this compound is that it burns the plants it's sprayed on extremely rapidly, usually leading to a dead-looking plant within a day or two. Unfortunately, this herbicide doesn't affect plants' roots—that is, it's a contact poison but not a systemic poison—so treated weeds can grow back.

I personally have used this pesticide alone and in a formulation with Roundup (glyphosate, a systemic herbicide). Pesticide companies often mix contact and systemic herbicides together in order to get the quick "burn down" that the contact herbicide offers as well as the excellent efficacy of the systemic herbicide, which will kill the plant at its roots. Often this mix is effective, but in certain situations, such as on hot days, the contact herbicide can really mess up how effectively the systemic herbicide works. This was my experience when I sprayed pelargonic acid mixed with Roundup on a very hot day: I found that the pelargonic acid killed the leaves it was sprayed on before the glyphosate could be taken up by the plant through its leaves and from there moved through the plant's stem to the roots, meaning that the leaves that were sprayed died but the root system survived and the plant came back. This is actually a lesson taught in most pesticide application courses: be very careful if you're applying a contact poison (pelargonic acid) and a systemic poison (glyphosate) at the same time, because the contact poison may inhibit the systemic poison by too quickly killing the leaves that need to be present for the systemic poison to be absorbed by the plant.

 Pelargonic acid burns plants down very rapidly. Wilting can sometimes be observed as soon as an hour or two after application if the day is very hot.

DRAWBACKS This chemical kills the tops of plants and not the bottoms.

THE BOTTOM LINE This herbicide is good at burning down plants but not as good at killing the whole plant. If this pesticide is used in conjunction with a systemic herbicide that kills plants at the root, such as glyphosate, it may inhibit it by preventing the systemic herbicide from being absorbed because it burns the leaf so quickly. This is mostly a concern in very hot weather. I prefer to use my glyphosate straight, without this or other active ingredients mixed in.

Sodium chloride

The idea of using salt, or sodium chloride, to control weeds was one of J. I. Rodale's favorites. In his book *The Organic Front*, his words describing the concept of presalted celery verge on poetry. Presalted celery was actually patented by Nick Engel, a farmer in Wisconsin, in 1945 and involved applying one thousand pounds of salt per acre prior to planting.

By and large we don't use salt as an herbicide much anymore, with good reason. Salt can hang out in the soil and damage future crops in some situations and may also affect the ecosystem of the soil, because some microbes just don't like this compound. Still, salt can be a good herbicide in situations where the crop you're going to grow is resistant to it. Celery, as just noted, and asparagus are two such crops. Once this substance is applied, and especially if it's applied at a concentration of one thousand pounds per acre, it would be wise not to consider planting anything else there, at least until most of the salt has leached away.

 Salt is considered pretty safe with regard to human health. If your crops can handle it, it will certainly do a number on most weeds.

 Few crops are resistant to salt, and salt can damage future crops that are to be planted in the same area. Salt also affects soil microorganisms adversely.

If the crops you're growing can handle it, and if you're not planning to grow anything else for a while (probably two or three years), salt might be a good option for weed control for you. As a general rule, though, I'd stay away from it.

Solarization

If you were one of those young deviants who used a magnifying glass to fry ants, you know that the sun is hot and that this heat can be used to destroy life. Organic gardeners have at their disposal a way to harness the sun's energy in a way that's very similar. This process is called solarization. Experiments on solarization first conducted in Israel in 1974 showed that this practice has the potential to control harmful weeds, diseases, and insects in a patch of soil.

Solarization involves spreading clear plastic across an area to be cleared of living organisms including weeds and disease. The plastic allows light to go through it, heating the ground, but doesn't allow warm air to escape, kind of like a minigreenhouse without a cooling system. Solarized and unsolarized soils in the same location typically show a difference of about 16 degrees F (about 9 degrees C) (Katan 1981), but this can vary depending on climate. The heat produced will kill weed seeds as well as many plant pathogens that may live in the soil and infect root systems such as pythium, rhizoctonia, and verticillium.

If you're thinking of trying solarization, here are a few pointers. To be most efficient the plastic must be close to the ground, so any weeds or grass in the area should be mowed down as low as possible (two inches or so will work) or removed prior to applying the plastic. Solarization can also be accomplished on ground that has been tilled. The plastic should be applied during the hot part of the year and it should stay in place for four to six weeks to make sure you kill off the stuff that you want to get rid of. For cooler climates, such as Pennsylvania and points north, the length of time the plastic stays on the ground can be extended to get better control. That will mean that your ground will be covered with the plastic during a time when you might like to be growing things, but if it's soil-borne diseases that you're worried about, the good news is that the effects of solarization have in some cases lasted up to three years (Katan, Fishler, and Grinstein 1980). Though different sorts of plastic have been used for solarization, a thin, clear polyethylene plastic is generally best. The thinner the plastic the better the transmission of sunlight through it, and the cheaper it will be. Do be aware that polyethylene will break down from the very sunlight that you're encouraging to go through this plastic, and you shouldn't expect it to last for more than three years of use, or less in some cases.

BENEFITS Solarization will do a good job of knocking out weeds and plant pathogens in your garden without the use of chemicals.

DRAWBACKS Solarization knocks out mycorrhizae and other beneficial organisms as well as the not-so-beneficial ones. The length of time that the plastic needs to stay on the ground may limit the crops that can be grown in that location later in the year. This process works best in geographical locations that have a long, sunny, warm growing season. Finally, though most people would consider this process organic, plastic is a synthetic material.

BOTTOM LINE If you have recurring disease problems, solarization is a great idea despite the fact that depending on where you live, you may lose a year of gardening on the patch of land you solarize. It may also be a good idea for knocking down weed populations early in a season.

Vinegar (acetic acid)

Many organic herbicides are currently available that include high concentrations of acetic acid. These herbicides tend to be effective at killing the top portions of weeds and so make the weed appear dead. Unfortunately this "death" is usually short lived and the plant ends up coming back with a vengeance because its roots weren't killed. Vinegar is relatively safe at the concentrations used when preparing food, but once acetic acid concentrations get much above 5 percent or so, these sprays can be dangerous. Getting vinegar in your eye is no fun at all, and the higher the concentration of acetic acid the less fun it is.

BENEFITS Vinegar can do a good job of burning down weeds. It certainly acts quickly and it's very satisfying to see results so soon after an herbicide application.

DRAWBACKS Weeds that have well-established root systems will come back from their roots and you'll have to reapply, perhaps many times, to get control.

BOTTOM LINE Organic herbicides that contain a low concentration of acetic acid, such as vinegar, will do a good job of burning down weeds quickly, but reapplication will be necessary for plants with strong root systems.

Synthetic herbicides

A large assortment of synthetic herbicides can be extremely effective against weeds As we've seen, some organic herbicides are quite serviceable, but in general they don't stack up against synthetics in terms of effectiveness. Nonetheless, for maintaining the land these organic compounds can provide enough weed control for most gardeners who are willing to weed at least weekly.

As we begin looking at synthetic herbicides, consider yourself fore-warned that I'm not a fan of any of them as they can be extremely danger-ous. In my opinion, hand weeding is always the best choice for the gar-dener unless you've got a section of land that's simply so large that it is unmanageable without chemicals or you've got a specific perennial plant that you just haven't been able to kill any other way.

As mentioned earlier, herbicides can be either preemergence or poste-mergence, and they can affect either broad-leaved plants or grasses. Pre-emergence herbicides kill plants as they emerge from the seed. These her-bicides generally have a long residual, which means that they remain in the soil for a long period of time so that they can continue to affect new seeds as they fall on the ground. These products typically last from one to six months, depending on the chemical used and the type of soil it's applied to. Postemergence products affect plants after they break the surface of the soil. Broad-spectrum products like glyphosate must be applied with care to keep them away from the plants you're trying to keep alive. Other, more specific herbicides such as 2,4-D will kill only broad-leaved plants such as dandelions and clover and not your lawn or corn (a type of grass), while certain grass herbicides, such as sethoxydim, will kill grasses without hurt-ing your pansies or geraniums.

Broad-spectrum weed killers

Most of the herbicides used to clear land fall into the category of broad-spectrum postemergence weed killers. Basically all that means is that these poisons are intended to kill a wide variety of plants that have already sprouted from the soil. The most common of these that you're likely to see or use are glyphosate and glufosinate-ammonium. Glyphosate and glufos-inate-ammonium are probably the safest herbicides to use when preparing ground for planting because of their ability to kill most weeds while main-taining a short life in the soil; once these products are applied, they're quickly neutralized by natural degradation processes or by adsorption to soil particles and cease to have much effect on plants. In contrast to this are a number of preemergence herbicides such as trifluralin that last for a long time after they're applied to the soil and that are likely to affect the plants you want to save (especially when they're being started in the ground as seeds) as well as the weeds you want to kill.

Besides their short lives in the soil, glyphosate and glofosinate-ammonium are relatively safe for humans and the environment if they're used in accordance with their labeled instructions. The EIQs for glyphosate and glufosinate-ammonium are 15.3 and 28.2, respectively. Recall that EIQs can range from a high of about 100 to a low of about 10. To me, any score of less than 20 looks pretty good. The score of 28 isn't bad but is starting to get into the range where I, personally, begin to look for something with a lower EIQ if one is available that will do the same job.

A number of organic growers out there would consider my statement that these chemicals are relatively safe heresy, and they have some cause for this because scientific articles on glyphosate have been published that seem to indicate that this product is quite dangerous. Studies have shown that glyphosate can have detrimental effects on the environment, or on people, and some will point to these studies as a justification for their revulsion at all that's synthetic. I'm not one of these people, but I do think it's worth the time to look at a few of these studies and investigate what they actually mean. The first and least damning of these studies, conducted by Lennart Hardell and Mikael Eriksson, came out in 1999. This study supposedly showed that the use of glyphosate was associated with the onset of non-Hodgkin's lymphoma and was touted as proof that Roundup (whose active ingredient is glyphosate) is an evil pesticide that should never be used. The authors didn't say this, mind you; rather, people involved in organics took ahold of this paper and made it into something big. The results showed a high-odds ratio of 2.3 for the use of glyphosate, meaning in a nutshell that people who used glyphosate were 2.3 times more likely to develop non-Hodgkin's lymphoma than those who didn't use it at all. This could be a very significant finding, but before accepting this result as gospel we need to take a closer look at what, exactly, an odds ratio is and what other statistics go along with it.

An odds ratio is an indication of how likely it is that given exposure to something, you'll have an occurrence of a particular malady. An odds ratio of 1.0 means that if you're exposed to a particular chemical, you're as likely to get a specified malady as anyone else on the street; an odds ratio of 0 means that you'll never get the malady if you're exposed to the chemical; and an odds ratio greater than 1.0 means that you're more likely than the average person on the street to get the malady if you're exposed to the chemical. Given this information, it certainly looks like being exposed to glyphosate can lead to an increased chance of your getting non-Hodgkin's lymphoma.

The problem with the conclusions that people have leapt to regarding this study is that only four people out of the just over five hundred in the study got this disease, which is an extremely small number for a large statistical study, and it's entirely possible that this number of people could have developed non-Hodgkin's lymphoma just by chance. Furthermore, this study offered a confidence interval along with the odds ratio that tells a different story. A confidence interval is a measurement of how certain an odds ratio is. A narrow confidence interval, something like 2.0–2.6, would reveal that the given odds ratio is based on good solid evidence. A wide confidence interval, such as 0.5–10, would reveal that the odds ratio isn't particularly useful, and since the number 1.0 is contained in this range, it would actually demonstrate that there's little evidence that the chances of getting non-Hodgkin's lymphoma given exposure to glyphosate is any different from the chances of contracting non-Hodgkin's lymphoma given no exposure to glyphosate. The confidence interval for the odds ratio in this study was 0.4–13. This is a very large confidence interval, indicating that our confidence in the odds ratio should be quite low. Since this study was conducted, one other very large study investigated more than fifty-four thousand people exposed to various pesticides including glyphosate. This study turned up no evidence that glyphosate exposure had anything to do with non-Hodgkin's lymphoma and in fact showed no significant relationship between glyphosate use and any cancer (De Roos et al. 2005).

After reading about the last study you're probably getting the idea that I'm not overly concerned about the safety of glyphosate, but that isn't exactly true. An environmental study demonstrated that under some easily conceivable misapplication scenarios, Roundup or other glyphosate products could have deleterious effects on the environment. A researcher from the University of Pittsburgh, Rick Relyea, clearly found that frogs are quite susceptible to Roundup poisoning when it's applied in a heavy dose directly to the water-filled areas where they live (Relyea 2005). Relyea doesn't blame glyphosate for the toxicity of this product to frogs, though; he blames the inactive ingredients (basically soaps and oils) that the glyphosate is mixed with. Almost every pesticide includes inactive ingredients, including things such as soaps and oils, that help the pesticide to work but that aren't considered a pesticide in and of themselves. This is a problem because inactive ingredients can certainly have a hand in the effects that a particular compound might have on a person's health or on the environment. And this isn't the case only with synthetic pesticides; indeed, organic pesticides are also frequently formulated with inactive ingredients that also may affect unintentional targets. Currently, pesticide companies aren't required to list on their labels the inactive ingredients used.

The moral of this story is that you should use pesticides, both synthetic and organic, in a way that's consistent with their labels. We aren't surprised if a flame from a flamethrower, a common organic method of weed control, kills frogs, so why are we surprised that getting a heavy dose of Roundup does? Be careful with any pesticide you use. It says right on the label how to apply the pesticide that you've decided to purchase. This information is there for a reason—don't take it lightly.

Frequently glyphosate is mixed with other chemicals, including diuron (EIQ 20.5, may irritate the eyes and throat), diquat (EIQ 31.7, more toxic that glyphosate), and/or others, depending on the specific product. These mixtures are usually made to kill the tops of plants while the glyphosate works on the roots, or to provide some preemergence control of weeds. The addition of these other herbicides usually has the effect of making these sprays more dangerous. I prefer products containing glyphosate and nothing else. I don't mind waiting a few days for the weeds to die and I don't like to apply preemergence pesticides before I plant my crops.

 Nonselective synthetic herbicides do an effective job of clearing land of plants. The material that's killed may even provide mulch and help hold the soil if a no-till management strategy is used. Even if tilling is used, the dead vegetation will provide additional organic matter to the soil as long as it isn't removed.

 Synthetic herbicides can have detrimental effects on the environment and on human health if they're used improperly or thoughtlessly.

![THE BOTTOM LINE] For initially clearing an area to prepare it for a garden, broad-spectrum postemergence herbicides make a lot of sense. How-

ever, improper use of these products can have very serious consequences for local ecosystems and human health.

Grass and broad-leaf weed killers

The postemergence herbicides just described, glyphosate and glufosinate-ammonium, must be used with extreme care because if these get on the plants you're trying to encourage, you might inadvertently kill them. (At the time of this writing I'm bemoaning the loss of a beautiful columbine that I inadvertently got some glyphosate on.) The postemergence grass and broad-leaf weed killers I'm about to describe are more selective. These herbicides target weeds while leaving the plants you want to save more or less alone.

A few grass killers currently on the market for homeowners don't affect broad-leaved plants. These chemicals usually work by inhibiting the production of certain oils within the plant and so kill the plant very slowly. The most common of the grass killers that you're likely to see on the garden center shelf is sethoxydim (EIQ 27.5), though you may also see fluazifop-butyl (EIQ 44). These herbicides are very effective at killing grasses and only rarely hurt broad-leaved plants. The biggest drawback is that they do take a long time to kill plants, up to four weeks, and so are not the chemicals to be using if you want to get rid of weeds for the garden party this weekend. Generally these chemicals shouldn't be used around turfgrasses.

The chemicals monosodium methanearsonate or MSMA (EIQ 18) and calcium methanearsonate affect certain weed grasses, such as crabgrass, while leaving most turfgrasses alone. These chemicals can be quite effective, but if you happen to apply one of them to turfgrass that can't tolerate them, you may have problems. Be sure to read the labels carefully. Finally, if you use these compounds much you need to be aware that they include arsenic and can increase the levels of arsenic in your soil. Arsenic is not a good thing to have increased levels of. If you're going to use either of these compounds, use them very judiciously.

Anyone who has tried to keep a lawn free of broad-leaved weeds knows about these herbicides, even if they haven't used them. They have a distinctive smell and it's very easy to tell when they've recently been applied. Most of the herbicides we currently use as broad-leaf weed killers are synthetic auxins. Auxins are basically hormones that encourage growth (a little like plant steroids). When a plant is exposed to too much auxin, it can't figure out exactly how it should be growing and it ends up killing itself. Both grasses and broad-leaved plants use auxins; however, the auxins used as herbicides tend to affect broad-leaved plants to a much greater degree than grasses.

The most common broad-leaf weed killers include 2,4-D (EIQ between 15 and 20 for most of the common products), mecoprop or MCPP (EIQ 21), dicamba (EIQ 28), and triclopyr, which is, incidentally, probably the best chemical available for killing shrubby weeds like buckthorn, honeysuckle, and poison ivy. (If you buy triclopyr for this purpose make sure that you're purchasing a product that says on its label that it's for killing weeds such as these.) All of these compounds can damage grasses at high enough concentrations, but at recommended dosages most grasses will be safe. Besides being available in the grocery store and garden center, these compounds are also widely applied by lawn care companies.

Like glyphosate, these compounds have been implicated again and again as potentially cancer-causing and highly dangerous. Unlike glyphosate, however, these herbicides have actually been shown by some studies to be cancer-causing and highly dangerous. A number of studies reviewing the cancer rates of people exposed to these chemicals over time have shown that these pesticides might indeed lead to problems. The most incriminating studies have looked at people who were exposed to the chemical many years ago. This is significant because in those days dioxins were part of these herbicides. Dioxins are very potent carcinogens and are in fact thought to be the major player in the problems experienced by those who were exposed to Agent Orange (a combination of 2,4-D and 2,4,5-T, the latter of which is no longer legal) during the Vietnam war. More recent studies have shown that these products seem to be safe (Garabrant and Philbert 2002), but this is one place where I can understand the outcry from those who hate pesticide use. I keep my use of these products to an absolute minimum and rarely see a need for more than one application per year. (Some yard companies will recommend three or four—this is absolutely nuts.)

 Selective postemergence herbicides are very effective at accomplishing the task they're designed for.

DRAWBACKS Care must be taken during the application of these products because of the potential for spray drift to adversely affect the plants you're trying to protect. Who cares about getting rid of a little dandelion that's competing with your peppers if you've inadvertently killed the peppers too? Finally, I'm somewhat concerned about some health issues, particularly with 2,4-D.

THE BOTTOM LINE These are generally good products that are reasonably safe if used as directed, but use them judiciously. Having no dandelions in your yard isn't worth the potential danger of applying 2,4-D five times a year, especially not when a single application will do most of the job. It's not the end of the world if there are three dandelions in your front lawn.

Preemergence herbicides

Most preemergence herbicides are very broad-spectrum poisons, meaning that they'll affect many different types of weeds before they emerge from the ground. Some of the most commonly used are dithiopyr (EIQ 22), oxyfluorfen (EIQ 33.8), pendimethalin (EIQ 29.7), prodiamine (EIQ 16.2), siduron (EIQ 16.3), and trifluralin (EIQ 18.8). Of these, only siduron has a residual of less than thirty days; pendimethalin is next with a residual of one to two months, and all of the other compounds are likely to last three months or longer. These long residuals are a two-edged sword: the herbicide you paid good money for will give you your money's worth, but you have a long time to wait until the chemical wears off if you're concerned about its safety. The good news is that these compounds are considered relatively safe for humans, in large part because physiologically animals and plants are much different, and also because they're generally not very water soluble. Being insoluble in water means that a compound won't be washed away by rains and can't easily cross the skin barrier. Chemicals that are water soluble can cross the skin barrier relatively easily and so have a greater potential for affecting people or animals that they come into contact with.

Besides safety, another consideration in choosing a preemergence herbicide is how well the herbicide affects the weeds you want to control. Pendimethalin and prodiamine are considered to be most effective on grasses such as crabgrass and foxtails, though they will also have some effect on broad-leafed weeds such as dandelions and thistle. Siduron is also most effective on grasses but is a special case because it doesn't affect the seeds of many turfgrasses, instead being more effective on weed grasses. This rare combination makes it a popular product to apply when seeding a new lawn. Trifluralin, oxyfluorfen, and dithiopyr are a little better at controlling broad-leaf weeds such as thistle and dandelion but will affect weed grasses too.

One other preemergence herbicide you may see in stores is imazapyr. Imazapyr is a very effective preemergence and postemergence herbicide that nonselectively kills whatever plants it hits and can remain in the soil preventing new weeds from sprouting for up to a year. This herbicide has an EIQ of only 18. A commercial formulation of this chemical combined with another chemical has the best, and scariest, name for a pesticide I've ever heard: Sahara. This herbicide is simply more than most people need.

Though preemergence herbicides aren't supposed to affect plants larger than the smallest seedlings, this isn't always the case. I've rarely seen these products actually kill a large plant, but every year I treat some young plants with trifluralin to demonstrate to my pesticide class what this product can do to a root system. The plants don't die, but the root systems become distorted and parts may even swell up into what look like minisausages. As you would expect, this can affect the plants' growth. The moral of this story is: Be careful. Even though you may not realize it, any application of an herbicide could affect other plants. If you're using a preemergence herbicide it's a good idea to allow at least a few weeks between applying the herbicide and transplanting anything, and vice versa.

BENEFITS These chemicals are extremely effective at stopping plants from growing before they see sunlight.

DRAWBACKS These chemicals can damage your crop plants if they're used incorrectly.

THE BOTTOM LINE Preemergence herbicides tend to be relatively safe and I like to use them at the nursery that I run because of its size and their convenience. I rarely use these chemicals at home. They must be used judiciously, and for most gardens, hand weeding still makes more sense.

THE BEST CHOICES FOR YOU

In some cases it's hard to argue that using organic practices is better than using herbicides. For example, suppose you have a large piece of land where you want to start a garden. You could till the ground, but that would lead to soil erosion, would uncover new weeds that would soon compete with plants you're trying to grow, and would make the ground more susceptible to compaction. So why not apply glyphosate and allow the weeds you've killed to work as mulch? Or apply glyphosate and then plant intercrops to increase organic matter while you're growing your plants? To me it just makes sense.

Organic herbicides have their place. Corn gluten meal can certainly be an effective preemergence herbicide, though it's expensive and takes a few years (and a few applications) to work. Most of the organic post-emergence herbicides can be pretty effective if they're used on young plants. Older plants with strong root systems may well shrug them off, though, unless they're repeatedly reapplied. Excellent synthetic herbicides exist that are relatively safe for the environment when they're used properly. I wouldn't use them if I could avoid it just because of cost, but after that factor there are good reasons to use these chemicals as long as they're used judiciously and in accordance with their labels.

Most methods of preparing the land for a garden aren't inconsistent with the initial use of synthetic chemicals, such as glyphosate, to get rid of weeds. What about land that's covered in hedges or other brush that's in the way of your proposed garden? If you can go out there and dig them out with a sickle and hoe, I'd say go for it. It's great exercise and it provides an incredible amount of satisfaction. If it's going to be a war, though, why not use the glyphosate or glufosinate-ammonium products? These herbicides can make your job a lot easier as long as you're careful with them; don't apply them to areas near standing water or near plants of value. Some would argue with me, feeling that there's quite enough evidence that glyphosate and glufosinate-ammonium products are bad for humans and the environment. I respectfully disagree. There are plenty of other pesticides to wish a pox upon. Glyphosate doesn't even come close to the top of the chart.

5

Insect Control

When Rachel Carson wrote *Silent Spring* she was careful to convey that pesticides, even synthetic ones, aren't the root of all evil and shouldn't be banned but rather should be used wisely by skilled people. In her words, "It is not my contention that chemical insecticides must never be used. I do contend that we have put poisonous . . . chemicals into the hands of persons largely or wholly ignorant of their potentials for harm." She also was careful to point out that a wide variety of other ways to get rid of pests are available beyond simply using insecticides. From nematodes to insect diseases, a plethora of avenues exist to treat for insects without resorting to synthetic or organic insecticides. But why bother with insect control at all if you don't have to? One of my favorite ways to deal with pests is by ignoring them and instead concentrating on getting plants to grow as vigorously as possible. A healthy and growing plant is better able to tolerate insect damage than one that isn't and often eliminates the need for insecticides.

When deciding on a control strategy the educated gardener should keep in mind that both synthetic and organic insecticides work, and that both pose potential hazards to the user. The big difference between them is that organic controls include many more options than just pesticides, though plenty of those are available. Without a doubt, using methods other than insecticides is better for you and the environment than applying chemicals; however, most gardeners at one time or another want to apply an insecticide to get rapid control of a pesky insect. Before this happens it's easy for organic gardeners to say that they're being good stewards of the environment, but after this happens it may be more difficult, depending on what they decide to do. Using pesticides, whether organic or synthetic, is a tricky business and it isn't reasonable to assume that any pesticide is safe in a given situation without first doing your homework, which is where this chapter comes in.

Those who choose insecticides, be forewarned. The use of broad-spectrum insecticides (poisons that kill a wide array of insect pests), be they organic or synthetic, leads to the death of beneficial insects. Once these beneficial insects are gone, nothing can stop the bad guys from rebounding and attacking your garden—except more pesticides. In other words, insecticide applications beget insecticide applications. That doesn't mean that insecticide applications are always the wrong choice. It does mean that you need to take some time and really think about what you're doing. Choosing an insecticide should not be a quick trip to the store to snatch something or other off the shelf.

As you read about the various methods of getting the upper hand with insect pests, think about their safety and efficacy and ask yourself whether the controls are appropriate for you. Will they be effective enough in your situation? Will they be safe enough in your situation? Will they take too much time? After you're finished reading this section ask yourself whether the organic controls, particularly the nonpesticide controls, seem like they would be safer than and/or more effective than synthetic controls in the situations where you want to use them. Your answer to this question should tell you whether you want to consider using organic insect controls exclusively.

Organic cultural practices

You can choose from a wide range of organic practices to control insects, but my favorite by far is the "don't do anything" method. If you're growing healthy plants by keeping them well watered and fertilized, you're likely to have many fewer insect pests than if you're not. Besides, most plants can deal with the loss of about a third of their leaf area to insect pests before they start to suffer a severe reduction in growth or production.

The organic choices described here either don't involve poisons at all or use only minute quantities. Unfortunately, none of these controls is as foolproof as simply spaying toxic compounds, but then none is as danger-ous, either. Although it's fascinating and encouraging to see the number and types of nonpesticide controls for insects that have been developed, it pays to be realistic. Most poison-free controls must be planned and in place before insects need to be controlled. Once large populations of insects enter an area, few of the non–poison-based controls will have much effect, and those that might tend to be expensive and labor intensive.

Bagging fruit

Placing bags around fruit, usually apples, is a great way to go if you've got only a few fruit trees in the yard. You can buy commercially produced Japanese fruit bags that will block insects and diseases from getting to your fruit, or you can use clear sandwich bags. If you're working with apples, you'll want to put the bag over the fruit when it's almost the size of a quarter. Staple the top of the bag to hold it on and cut small holes in the bottom of the bag to allow rainwater to run out. Remove these bags just before the apples ripen to get the best color. Do be aware that although these bags are often very effective, they're not cure-alls and it's normal for a few fruits to be blemished.

 This is a very effective method of controlling insects that get into fruit and it also helps to control many diseases.

 This is a very labor-intensive practice and is usually not used for more than a few trees.

THE BOTTOM LINE If all you have is a few apple trees, this is a great idea. If you have a whole orchard, this control may be too much work.

Choosing naturally insect-resistant plants

One of the best routes when selecting plants for your garden is to select plants that are resistant to the insects you're most concerned about. No plant will be completely resistant to insect attack, of course, and no plant will be resistant to attacks from all insects, especially those plants that have been subjected to stress in some way. Nonetheless, many plants have been identified as having few insect pests, and a quick perusal of extension literature will reveal trees, shrubs, vegetables, and other plants that are more resistant to the insects that may infest plants in your area.

Sometimes you'll be looking for a plant that simply has few pests—for example, star anise. And sometimes you'll want to grow a particular type of plant that's known to have a specific problem and you'll be interested in choosing the variety that's least likely to have the problem—for example, if you want to plant a birch in your yard, the best choice is a river birch rather than a paper birch because of the resistance that river birch has to the bronze birch borer. You can achieve either of these goals by doing careful research before you go to the garden center, using online information provided by your local extension service. Do remember that resistance is not immunity. Just because a plant is resistant to a pest doesn't mean that it's immune to the problem. Stress caused by a lack of water or nutrients can lead to a decrease in resistance in even the most ironclad plants.

Many different insect-resistant plant species are produced at any given time, so it's best to review extension guides from your area to select the appropriate resistant plant for your purposes. Additionally, insect resistance of certain species may be high in some areas of the country and low in others because certain insects won't flourish in certain areas. Once again, it's best to check with your extension service to confirm which species will be most insect resistant in your area.

Although insect-resistant plants are generally considered safe for people to be around, there are exceptions, albeit uncommon ones. Resistance usually means an increase in plant-defensive chemicals, and although these chemicals are usually benign to humans, it's possible for them to cause problems. For example, people handling a new form of insect-resistant celery contracted rashes when exposed to sunlight as a result of the increased presence of a group of chemicals called psoralens in this plant (Ames, Profet, and Gold 1990).

BENEFITS Choosing insect-resistant species to grow is usually a safe and effective way to decrease feeding by pests. It's also incredibly easy to implement and requires almost no upkeep once the resistant plant is placed in the garden.

DRAWBACKS In rare cases, insect resistance will make a plant hazardous to humans because of the increased presence of defensive compounds in the plant. Insects can overcome plant resistance in some situations, the most notable being when plants are under heavy stress.

Insect-resistant plants are often more expensive than insect-susceptible plants.

THE BOTTOM LINE Though choosing insect-resistant plants is a great way to go, do be aware that a plant that's resistant to some insects won't be resistant to all insects and that even plants that are supposed to be resistant to a certain insect may succumb if put under stress.

Maintaining cleanliness

If you want to keep insects off of your plants, one thing you simply must do is to get rid of old fruit, fallen leaves, and failing plants. All of these things offer a safe haven for pest insects from which they can launch scavenging forays to your good plants. Many pests can live in fallen leaves and fruit and in dying trees.

Some people like to use fallen leaves as natural mulch under their trees. If you know that these trees have few disease and insect problems, there's nothing inherently wrong with this; however, if you're dealing with such plants as apple or peach trees, which can get a wide variety of foliar diseases and insects, this is a mistake. In general it's better to rake up your leaves and compost them well (effectively killing most pests) and then use them as a soil amendment rather than as a mulch.

Many gardeners pride themselves on being able to bring back a plant that seems close to death. These plants are usually not worth saving and cause more problems than they're worth. Various beetles, caterpillars, and other pests often attack these plants first and establish a "beachhead" from which they can attack your healthy plants. Get rid of them.

BENEFITS Your garden looks nicer and fewer pests hang around.

DRAWBACKS It takes a little time to clean up.

THE BOTTOM LINE To have a good garden you've got to get rid of diseased and dying plants as well as old fruit and uncomposted leaf litter to ensure that insects and disease don't take over.

Using floating row covers and Reemay

One method of keeping insects off of your plants that's about as close to 100 percent guaranteed as it gets in the garden is using a floating row cover. Just isolate your plants and cover them with something that can't be penetrated by insects, and you're home free. Unfortunately, covering your plants may also inhibit them from getting stuff they need like light, water, and fertilizer. Fortunately, there's Reemay, a type of polyester cloth that lets water and about 80 percent of light through. This cloth can be applied while plants are young and stay on for most of the growing season; it's lightweight enough that plants will actually push it upward as they grow. The edges of the cloth are usually held down with soil, rocks, or something similar so that pests can't sneak in under the fabric. One warning: it's entirely possible that a few bad insects will get through the cloth at some point; if so, they'll be well protected from predators and will attack your crops with abandon. So be wary of this and don't assume that just because you're using Reemay your crops are completely safe. This product is also supposed to protect against light frosts and even mammalian pests like mice and rabbits.

BENEFITS It's tough to get through solid barriers, and if things go right, this stuff can really help with almost any pest you can name (though I have my doubts about how long rodents would be kept out if they were really hungry).

DRAWBACKS I really wouldn't expect mice and rabbits to be controlled for too long if they were especially hungry, and insect pests that do find their way into this structure might cause a great deal of damage as they cavort under the Reemay safe from predators. Floating row covers won't control weeds, so you'll need to remove these covers once in a while to get rid of these unwelcome guests. Additionally, the reduction in light that Reemay causes could reduce plant growth. Finally, this product isn't, strictly speaking, organic—it's a synthetic plastic.

THE BOTTOM LINE Reemay is good stuff that deserves to be used more, but do be aware that pests can get inside and cause damage.

Handpicking and hosing

Time to get down and dirty. Two methods of ridding your plants of insects include very personal contact with the insects: picking them off by hand and spraying them off with a hard stream of water.

Handpicking is a great way to get rid of big, and if your garden is small enough, little insects. This method requires nothing more than getting down on your hands and knees and squeezing the tar out of the bad bugs until they pop. This can become messy, so gloves are a good idea. I know some people who like to remove insects without squishing them, and that's OK, but you'll run the risk of having that insect come back.

The hose method is somewhat less personal. Just spray your plants with a hard stream of water to wash the rascals off. This method doesn't guarantee the death of the insects you hit with the hose, but it's a lot easier than handpicking, meaning that you can treat more plants in a shorter period of time. Do be careful with that stream of water, though; if the stream is too hard you might pressure wash the leaves right off of your plants. Sure, that'll get rid of the bugs, but wasn't it the leaves you were trying to save in the first place?

BENEFITS Physically removing insects with your hands or water certainly doesn't use any toxic chemicals, and these techniques can be quite effective.

DRAWBACKS It takes more time to spray or pick a bug off than to poison it, and if you use the handpicking method you may get bug blood on your hands.

THE BOTTOM LINE If you've got only a few plants and have a little time, these are great methods, but you'll probably need to use them repeatedly over the course of a season. One squishing usually doesn't do the trick, in my experience.

Providing nectaries

How about setting out a little snack for any beneficial insects that are thinking of dropping by? Maybe a tasty little appetizer to keep them happy until they find something else to eat? Many of the beneficial insects that show up in your garden can be enticed to stick around and take care of other less-than-desirable insects by the presence of nectar, which is usually found in flowers but may also be present in other parts of the plant. Many of these beneficial insects use pollen and/or nectar as an alternate food source and some actually feed on nectar at one stage of their life (usually the adult stage) and pests at another.

Among the greatest allies you have in your fight against insect pests are the parasitic wasps that occur naturally in your garden. These parasitic wasps are similar to, and may be the same as, the parasitic wasps you can purchase. Many of these wasps feed on pest insects while they're larvae and on nectar when they become adults. Having a lot of flowers around won't entice as many wasps to enter your garden as you could buy, but the flowers will serve to keep those wasps that you purchase closer to your garden as well as enticing wasps that might be planning on just passing through to stay awhile. Other beneficial insects that may be enticed to stay in your garden through the use of nectaries include big-eyed bugs, minute pirate bugs, ladybugs, and lacewings. Nectaries aren't a cure-all and they won't bring in enough beneficial insects to suddenly make your garden into a house of horrors for aphids, but they're a good way to foster biological control in your garden in an aesthetically pleasing way.

Most flowering plants that we think of as attractive, such as gardenias, camellias, marigolds, roses, and even things like dandelions and thistle can help to draw beneficial insects into a garden. But even plants that don't put on an incredibly showy floral display like dill and fennel may be attractive to parasitic wasps and other beneficial insects and could help to increase their numbers in the garden (Patt, Hamilton, and Lashomb 1997).

BENEFITS Having plants that produce nectar in your garden increases its biological diversity and makes it more attractive. Including nectaries in your garden is certainly cheaper than buying in beneficial insects.

DRAWBACKS Despite increasing the number of nectaries in your garden, sometimes you just don't bring in enough beneficial insects to control all of the pests.

BOTTOM LINE Why not use nectaries? I simply can't think of one good reason. Most of us use them in our gardens without even knowing it.

Planting polycultures and companion plants (intercropping)

Planting polycultures to prevent insects from becoming established is one of the best means of providing protection to your garden that there is. This method is pretty straightforward and can be summed up in one sentence: Don't plant the same types of plants next to each other. When you do, you offer insects the opportunity to eat their fill of one plant and then simply move on to the one next to it. Companion planting is a type of polyculture where a particular plant is planted beside a crop plant to repel critters from the crop plant.

All sorts of lists appear in various books that present particular companion plants for particular crops, and some of these are very good, but some are based on little more than ideas from the top of the author's head. The key to companion planting is simple. Make sure that similar plants aren't placed next to each other. For example, tomatoes and potatoes are closely related, so planting them together isn't a good idea. Some garden experts do recommend planting like plants next to each other because like plants will share similar nutrient, light, and watering requirements. While this is generally true, I firmly believe that in a garden situation avoiding pests is more important than meeting growth requirements perfectly, so I steer away from planting like plants together.

If you're looking for a list of plant companions, I must apologize because I'm not going to offer it here, in large part because I don't want you to get bogged down by thinking that one plant *must* be planted beside another. Just plant things that are different together and you'll reduce pest problems. But if you really want a book that lists companions, I'll point you to the popular *Carrots Love Tomatoes* by Louise Riotte. I think her companion choices make lots of sense, though I'll also admit that I'm not sold on many of her other ideas, such as herbal sprays. Here's a quick lesson. No book, this one included, is going to have all of the answers and get it all right. Do your best to research everything, read different opinions, and pay careful attention to the results of every garden practice you employ.

Then take the good and reject the bad. I like to think that I do a pretty good job of providing the basics, but sometimes you've just got to try stuff for yourself.

In my opinion some of the best research on companion planting was conducted by Stan Finch, Helen Billiald, and Rosemary Collier (2003). They looked at whether aromatic plants, those most commonly recommended by organic gardeners to repel bad bugs, are more effective than other sorts of plants at repelling the cabbage root fly and the onion fly. Why, you may ask, is it so important to look at the cabbage root fly and the onion fly and not something like whiteflies and aphids? The reason is that they're relatively large and in control of where they go. Small insects like whiteflies and aphids pretty much go where the wind takes them. That's not to say they don't have places they want to go that they can't make it to on a nice calm day, but in general they have a tough time fighting the wind. Planting a mix of plants will definitely slow down these little pests simply because plants they don't like will get in the way of their arriving at the plants they do like.

But back to the cabbage root fly and the onion fly, two insects that have plenty of control over where they're going. What Stan Finch and his partners discovered is that these flies seem to key on a chemical marker first (the fragrance of the plant they want to eat wafting through the air), then a physical marker (such as color or shape of leaves), then, after the insect lands, the flavor of the leaf. That means that once the flies are within sight of a plant, they'll be confused by other plants in the area (they're all green, after all) and will often land on these other plants. Since these flies have a small host range (they don't feed on a whole lot of different types of plants), they won't be happy about landing on the wrong plant (which they'll be able to tell by tasting it) and will move on, perhaps missing the plant you want to protect. Nice work—your companion planting paid off.

Finch's research investigated a large number of plants as companion plants, including highly fragrant plants. Highly fragrant plants are, of course, those plants that are advertised as being able to disrupt insects from reaching your tomatoes (or other crops) by screwing up their ability to locate host plants. The researchers found that the presence of a strong aroma didn't necessarily correlate to plants being more effective as companions. In fact, color seemed to be the best indicator of whether a plant would be an effective companion. The least effective companion plants were those that were a different color (grayish) from the plants that the insects were looking for.

One of the toughest insects to confuse appears to be the Japanese beetle. In a study investigating the effects of planting rue, zonal geranium, and garlic chives around roses to protect them from Japanese beetles, the beetles either weren't psyched out by the other crop or were encouraged to become more numerous on the roses (geraniums increased Japanese beetle populations). In a test conducted by the same researchers (Held, Gonsiska, and Potter 2003), bags of fragrant plants were placed around roses in an attempt to confuse the Japanese beetles through scent disruption. Guess what? Just as with the live plants, the Japanese beetles saw right through the researchers' little ruse, and populations of Japanese beetles were just as high on plants "protected" with bags of crushed red pepper, fennel seeds, crushed spearmint, cedar shavings, Osage orange fruits, and fleshy ginkgo seeds as on unprotected plants.

BENEFITS Planting polycultures is easy and the benefits can be great. If you're planting a small garden, just mixing up the things you grow is going to help limit damage by insect pests.

DRAWBACKS For pests such as the Japanese beetle that like to eat everything, this may not be the most effective method of control and may in some cases make matters worse. Companion planting isn't used by commercial producers in part because it's more difficult to harvest things that are different from each other than it is to harvest things that are the same, primarily because they ripen at different times. So if you have a very large garden, it may be more time consuming for you to harvest if you use companion planting methods.

THE BOTTOM LINE For anyone planting an acre or less, there's every reason to use companion planting. Do be aware that just because a plant is aromatic doesn't mean that it's more effective at repelling pests. In fact, the aroma can make things worse.

Traps and barriers

So you're having trouble getting rid of insects. Hey, why not give them what they want? If you can provide food or a suitable mate, or at least make it seem like you're providing food or a suitable mate, maybe you can lure your enemy in and then sock it to them with some kind of poison or barrier that doesn't let them out, at least not until they're dead.

Pheromones, attractive structures, and baits comprise some of the best ways to take care of troublesome insects without using chemicals (or with minimal chemical use). Traps are usually targeted toward one particular type of insect, based on the specific tastes of that insect. With that in mind, I've listed some of the most common traps for insects below along with some information on how effective they are and how they can best be used. Though these traps are usually considered organic, many of them include chemicals such as pheromones that are produced synthetically.

Ant traps

Ant traps are usually little round disks with holes cut into the sides for ants to enter and exit. These traps usually contain some kind of bait to entice the ants to enter as well as some sort of poison that will eventually kill them. The types of poisons used in ant traps can vary widely and may include organic or synthetic pesticides, but most of the poisons are intended to kill slowly so that the ant will bring it back to the nest to poison even more ants. Ant traps tend to be effective but need time to work. Don't expect an ant trap to clear out a population in a day. If you want the safest type of poison, you probably want traps that use boric acid, which unfortunately is also one of the slowest acting.

BENEFITS Ant traps are safer than spraying a poison because the poison stays inside the trap instead of being broadcast. Since the poison usually acts slowly, more of the ant nest is destroyed than if the poison acted quickly and killed the ant before it could return to its nest.

DRAWBACKS Ant traps, especially those that use boric acid, kill a nest of ants very slowly. I've personally had limited success with boric acid ant traps.

Ant traps are a relatively safe way to deal with ants. But do ask yourself whether the ants are really being that much of a nuisance. Most people kill ants because they're there and not because they're actually doing anything harmful. I prefer to save my wrath for insects that deserve it (which would, admittedly, include fire ants).

Japanese beetle traps

In regions of the country where Japanese beetles are found, a hot item is the Japanese beetle trap. These traps use a bait comprised of a female Japanese beetle hormone and/or a sweet-smelling food lure. These two compounds will attract Japanese beetles very effectively to an area. Unfortunately, simply attracting Japanese beetles to an area may not be a great thing. The apparatus used for catching Japanese beetles is usually a funnel into which the beetles fall after hitting a wall mounted on top of the funnel. At the bottom of the funnel is a bag that may have some sort of chemical to kill the beetle. The basic problem with these traps is that there are just too many Japanese beetles in most areas where people are using them. A trap can attract a huge number of Japanese beetles, but since the trap usually isn't capable of holding, or even trapping, all of the beetles it attracts, what often happens is that more beetles end up in your yard. In fact, where traps are placed next to trees, those trees generally suffer greater damage than trees without traps around. More traps usually means more damage (Gordon and Potter 1985, 1986).

But these traps can actually be quite useful to you despite this little problem. Do you have a neighbor who annoys you? Someone on whose house you wish a plague? Just give them a Japanese beetle trap for their birthday or some other convenient holiday and watch the nasty critters fly from your house to theirs. Actually, I have heard of situations where people are somewhat successful at controlling these beetles through the use of traps. These situations occur where a person owns a large piece of property and spreads these traps all over, almost to the point where you can't go fifty feet without bumping into one. I can't say that I've tried this myself, and I can't say that I ever want to.

BENEFITS The idea of sending all of your Japanese beetles over to your neighbor's yard with one of these traps has a certain comic appeal, even if you can't bring yourself to carry out this plan. If multiple traps are used on a large parcel of land, it's possible that some beneficial effect could be realized.

 In most situations these traps just don't catch enough beetles compared to the number they attract to be useful.

 Personally, I'd try something else.

Pheromone traps

In the movies there's nothing like sex to lure victims to their doom. But it's not only humans that get caught up in following sex to the point of getting themselves killed; insects will do it, too. Pheromone traps release odors that attract insects to the trap to be caught. The odors are usually chemical signals that a female releases to attract a male but may also be odors that signal the presence of food. Though a variety of insects can be caught with these traps, the insects you're most likely to buy these traps to control are the peach tree borer and the codling moth.

Borers are the most terrifying insects for owners of shrubs, trees, and perennials. These insects enter the plant through the bark and then set up residence inside the stems or trunk. Feeding on this sensitive area of a tree, borers can have serious effects and can actually lead to the tree's untimely demise. The peach tree borer is a particularly aggressive pest that can badly damage a peach tree. The codling moth is a major pest of apples but won't kill a tree like a borer can. Codling moths attack the apples themselves and make them particularly uninviting to those who might want to eat them.

In general, pheromone traps aren't considered to be as effective as spraying chemicals to control insects, but they can be somewhat effective if you have only small populations of moths. If you have just a tree or two that you're trying to protect and you're near a large orchard, be aware that this is a situation where these controls are unlikely to work. Large producers of fruit use pheromone traps as a way to tell when a particular pest is present in an orchard so that insecticidal sprays can be timed and useless sprays can be avoided. In smaller orchards, or when you have only one or two trees, the pheromone traps may work if you use one or two traps per tree, but this may get too expensive for your tastes.

The pheromone traps that you can purchase typically consist of two components, a cardboard or paper sheet that includes a sticky substance and an odor component that has the chemical that attracts the insect. Since pheromone traps attract primarily males, you've got to set these things out to catch or confuse the males before they have a chance to mate with the females. Once they mate with the females, the females will be able to lay their fertilized eggs on the plants or fruits you want to protect.

BENEFITS Pheromone traps can work in areas where you have small numbers of insects and where outside populations of pests, perhaps from a nearby orchard, aren't around to come into your yard. They're certainly a great way to find out whether you have a particular pest.

DRAWBACKS If you have a large population of the pests you're trying to get rid of, or if you're near an area that has a large, uncontrolled infestation of these pests, these traps just won't offer the control you need. It's a little nitpicky, but the baits used in these traps are synthetic chemicals.

THE BOTTOM LINE These are great tools for figuring out whether you have a particular pest and for timing pesticide applications so that you're sure to get the pest when it's around, but unless conditions are perfect these products all by themselves aren't great for controlling insects.

Sticky cards and paste

Some great products rely on the concept of using color to attract insects and sticky surfaces to catch them once they've been roped in. These products are called sticky cards and resemble index cards that have been covered with an annoyingly sticky substance. They're colored either yellow to attract aphids and fungus gnats or blue to attract thrips. Sticky cards are usually used in greenhouses, where small insects have more control over where they fly than in outdoor environments where they're largely directed by wind. Typically used to detect when pest numbers are increasing in a structure in order to schedule pesticide applications, these cards can also be used as a way to control these insect pests if enough are used in a small area. For use as a control, two sticky cards generally need to be placed in a container six inches in diameter with the sticky cards adjusted so that they're even with the canopy of the plant to be protected. I've used this method in the past to successfully control fungus gnats where I couldn't use pesticides (because of an experiment) and generally I was quite happy with it, but it sure wouldn't have won any awards for being attractive. This method uses a heckuva lot of sticky cards, and it does get to be quite a mess, with your hands invariably coated in a layer of annoying sticky goo (unless you wear rubber gloves), but it's a safe way to control these pests.

Besides sticky cards, sticky pastes can also be purchased that can provide protection from a variety of different insects, depending on how the paste is used and how carefully it's applied. One technique that's very time consuming but that can provide some protection from mites and aphids is spreading this paste along petioles and stems (not leaves) of plants to be protected. As insects attempt to move along the plant, they get caught in the paste and stopped.

BENEFITS The sticky paste that you can buy from the store is relatively nontoxic. If you're willing to spread as much of this stuff as you'll need, sticky cards and paste can be quite effective. There's nothing quite like looking at the sticky cards you placed out in the garden and seeing the little suckers that had been trying to eat your beans stuck to them.

DRAWBACKS This stuff is really messy.

THE BOTTOM LINE Sticky cards and pastes aren't a bad thing to try. In fact, they're great if you're just monitoring pest numbers. But they're so messy in most situations that they're just not the best option. Add in the time it takes to apply the paste and this stuff may begin to seem like quite a pain. I like these techniques for a plant or three, but for a whole garden? No way.

Visual traps (apple maggot and plum curculio traps)

A few types of traps available are based on insects' reactions to what they see. Just as we're drawn to the sight of a big steak, grilled shrimp, or a nice plate of hummus, insects in our gardens are drawn to shapes that represent food, and we can use this to our advantage. Two visual traps are used with some frequency by gardeners: the plum curculio trap and the apple maggot trap.

If you grow peaches (or apricots or plums) and have weevil problems, you've probably got the dreaded plum curculio. Most people first encounter this pest when they bite into a piece of fruit and find a worm inside. The worm isn't really a worm, though; it's actually the larvae of the plum curculio weevil. This pest is responsible for more insecticide sprays on peaches than any other single insect. In the 1990s a trap called the Tedders' trap was developed to catch this pest but was primarily used as a way to time sprays rather than as a way to actually control the problem. Orchardists would put out their trap and then wait until a plum curculio appeared in it before they started spraying. This trap is set up as two interlocking boards that are cut as triangles and that fit together so that when they're connected they're freestanding, with the points of the boards facing upward. At the pinnacle of these boards, about three feet from the ground, is a small cage into which insects crawl and where they become trapped. Though this trap is intended primarily for the plum curculio, other weevils and even spiders (I've seen black widows in these traps) will also find their way in. The reason this trap is so effective is that the plum curculio sees it and, being an insect with a very small brain, mistakes it for a tree. The insect then climbs up the trap, hoping to find some nice fruit on which to lay its eggs. Instead it finds a little tunnel that it crawls through. Unfortunately for the insect, this tunnel leads not to fruit but instead to a wire or plastic cage that may contain poison.

Apples are usually subjected to insecticide sprays for one of two reasons: the codling moth and the apple maggot. These pests have caused growers to apply all kinds of insecticides over the years to keep these fruits in a marketable state. A trap called the Ladd trap can reduce the number of insecticide applications needed by telling the orchard grower when to apply sprays for the apple maggot. This trap is nothing more than a round red ball that attracts apple maggot flies because they mistake it for an apple and then catches them in a sticky substance on the ball's surface. These traps may also include an attractive scent that may increase catches by quite a bit (MacCollom et al. 1994). If I were trying to use these lures to control the apple maggot, I would definitely buy scented lures.

Both the plum curculio trap and the apple maggot trap are used by growers primarily to help them time their insecticide applications so that they won't be spraying poisons needlessly, but both of these traps can also be used by gardeners to control pests. Unfortunately, not enough testing has been done for anybody to say conclusively how well these traps work when used alone for insect control.

BENEFITS Visual traps will capture some harmful insects and will certainly tell you when the pest insects that you're worried about controlling are around, as long as you pay attention. I've heard some success stories from gardeners who have used these traps to control pests without insecticides, but I've heard of some failures, too.

DRAWBACKS These traps haven't been fully tested at the garden level, so it's difficult to tell exactly how effective they are in different circumstances.

THE BOTTOM LINE If you have only a few trees, these traps are a good idea to try, but you also might consider just putting bags around your fruit after they reach the size of a quarter or so.

Beneficial insects and other organisms

A number of beneficial insects are offered for sale to the gardener, a few of which are very effective and a few of which might better be left alone. Without doubt, beneficial insects are a useful part of any garden and qualify as an organic way to control pests, but in most cases if care is taken when planting and growing, additional beneficial insects shouldn't be needed as they should already be there.

The best way to conserve beneficial insects in your garden is to avoid broad-spectrum insecticides (insecticides that kill insects indiscriminately). Most of the insecticides that you're likely to purchase, be they organic or synthetic, are broad-spectrum poisons that will devastate your population of beneficial insects and inhibit them from reentering the area until the poisons have broken down, which may take two weeks or more. Besides avoiding these broad-spectrum sprays, the best way to encourage beneficial insects is to plant flowers that contain nectar attractive to them (see the earlier section on nectaries). If you do decide to go the route of adding beneficial insects to your garden, you should be aware of the benefits and drawbacks of these little beasts. All beneficial insects are not created equal.

Lacewings

Lacewings are a little-known and underutilized predator. Lacewing adults are very pretty with green bodies and gossamer wings, but it's their ugly larvae that are effective at killing pests. When you purchase lacewings you usually get eggs, though larvae or adults may also be shipped. Eggs and larvae are generally preferred because the larvae that hatch from these eggs can't migrate out of your garden. Lacewing larvae look like tiny alligators and are incredibly voracious, eating mites, aphids, whiteflies, and other pests. In fact, I once held one of these guys on my finger as it attempted to eat a bit of melted chocolate on a warm day. I was surprised that during the five minutes that I held it, the minuscule chocolate puddle (about a tenth the size of the insect) actually did grow noticeably smaller.

 I love lacewings for a variety of reasons, not the least of which is that when you buy lacewing eggs, the hatching larvae won't leave your garden before they do their feeding.

 Lacewings, like ladybugs and most other beneficial insects, aren't compatible with insecticides. Although these creatures tend to stay where they're placed, they'll fly away when they become adults.

THE BOTTOM LINE Lacewings are a good choice for controlling aphids, mites, and other small soft-bodied insects.

Ladybugs

An extraordinary number of different types of ladybugs, also known as ladybeetles and ladybird beetles, exist in the world. Most ladybugs are predators and so are valuable to the gardener, with a few exceptions such as the Mexican bean beetle, which can actually be a devastating pest. On the shelf over my computer I have a 912-page book (actually it's an issue of the *Journal of the New York Entomological Society*) written by Robert Gordon and published in 1985 that looks at the 475 species of ladybugs in North America north of Mexico. Obviously all of these different types of ladybugs aren't for sale, but many of them can have a positive effect on your garden by feeding on insects that feed on your plants. The best advice I have for someone who wants to keep ladybugs in their garden is to stop spraying insecticides. Sure, that might mean that you'll have to put up with some insect problems for a season, but in time these fabulous insects will come back and you'll be happier for it.

Because of the carnivorous nature of most ladybugs, they've been a favorite subject for scientists who want to introduce a predatory insect into an area to take care of a particular problem. The first truly effective introduced biological control in the United States was a ladybug called the vedalia beetle that was brought into Florida in 1888–89 to attack cottony cushion scale, which was accidentally introduced into the United States in 1867 from Australia and which was devastating citrus orchards. The vedalia beetle proved to be so effective that by the end of 1889 cottony cushion scale ceased to be a major problem in citrus production. Interestingly enough, the use of DDT as a pest control in the 1940s and 1950s actually caused an outbreak of cottony cushion scale because of its effect on the vedalia beetle (DeBach and Bartlett 1951).

Not every ladybug introduction has had the same level of success as the vedalia beetle. Around 1980 the Asian ladybug, *Harmonia axyridis*, was introduced across the United States to feed on various insect pests, most notably aphids that attack pecans. Though this ladybug is effective at controlling pecan aphids, it has become something of a pest itself because of its propensity for flying into homes and setting up residence where it isn't wanted. I recently saw a TV show where a gentleman (who shall remain nameless) accused this beetle of not being a true ladybug and of causing a great deal of damage to homes. This gentleman is completely wrong. *Harmonia* is a true ladybug that does all of the good things that ladybugs do. It can't directly harm your home, but in the fall these insects do look for protected locations to spend the winter and so will take up residence in houses and make themselves into a nuisance, but they won't actually hurt anything (unless you get frustrated and smash them against the drapes— they will stain). It's true, however, that the Asian ladybug will feed on fruits and vegetables that are overripe or damaged, and sometimes even healthy raspberries and other thin-skinned fruits, so it's only fair to say that this ladybug can be a minor garden pest.

For most gardeners, the ladybugs that are naturally in their gardens are sufficient to control most pests, and adding more ladybugs isn't warranted. If you do want to try adding ladybugs, you'll probably purchase either *Hippodamia convergens*, aka the convergent ladybeetle, or *Cryptolaemus montrouzieri*, better known as the mealybug destroyer. Both of these ladybugs are good at eating. Unfortunately, the convergent ladybeetle has a tendency to leave the area where it was released (Rankin and Rankin 1980), making it a somewhat unreliable predator. The mealybug destroyer is less likely to leave if sufficient prey are available and is frequently released into conservatories and other enclosed spaces from which it can't escape.

BENEFITS Ladybugs are fantastic eaters, especially when they're larvae. Different species of ladybugs will attack mealybugs, aphids, mites, young caterpillars, scale, and other pests.

DRAWBACKS Ladybugs have a tendency to leave. Because they're collected while hibernating, they have a desire to disperse as soon as they're released. Certain ladybugs are advertised as being more likely to stick around your garden after release, but these claims haven't been tested adequately for me to endorse them.

THE BOTTOM LINE If you've got an enclosed area where you're releasing ladybugs, they ought to do fine, but if you're releasing them into an open area, they may well leave before they have a chance to do much good. Perhaps the most important thing to know about ladybugs is that they're very susceptible to insecticides. If you're planning on using insecticides, don't plan on buying ladybugs. Personally, I'm not a believer in purchasing ladybugs for outdoor situations and instead try to concentrate on conserving the ladybugs I have naturally through reduced use of insecticides.

Praying mantis

The praying mantis is a fantastically beautiful insect that's a joy to see in your garden but that's not particularly effective at controlling insect pests. Yes, it's a predator and will certainly attack some of your pest insects. The problem is that the mantis is too big and these insects don't tend to congregate together in large numbers, reducing their efficacy.

 The praying mantis is a big insect, so it can attack larger insects than those that many of the other beneficials will take on.

 This insect doesn't eat enough per mantis to be a particularly effective predator for the gardener's purposes.

A mantis is a beauty to behold, but in terms of controlling insect pests it's all flash and no substance. It's one I rejoice in seeing but not one I'd consider buying.

Minute pirate bugs and big-eyed bugs

The minute pirate bug and the big-eyed bug are two of the best predators that you can buy. They both have voracious appetites and a similar size. These insects are my favorite predators and are known to attack thrips, mites, aphids, young caterpillars, and many other pests. One nice trait that these guys have is that while they can fly, they tend to stay around your garden as long as something is available for them to eat. But don't think that this means that you can't release these predators if you don't see any pests. They also feed on pollen, so if you have some flowers blooming and want to release these insects to defend against something that you suspect could pop up in the near future, go for it—they can survive on pollen until the pests show up.

 These insects eat a wide range of pests, and because they tend to stick around they can offer pest control for a significant period of time. If enough pests aren't available these insects can find alternate food sources.

 These insects can and will fly away in situations where their appetites can't be satiated.

These beneficial insects are a great choice in almost any situation.

Nematodes

Little worms that eat insects from the inside out are a great choice for any garden if the situation is appropriate for their success. Nematodes are most effective at controlling insects that spend some portion of their time living in the soil, such as the Japanese beetle. These worms can actually kill up to 80 percent of a pest population under the right circumstances, which includes a moist soil and a comfortably warm temperature (greater than about 60 degrees F). Nematodes are able to tolerate most commonly used insecticides much better than most beneficial insects, so using these pesticides won't necessarily destroy the usefulness of this biological control (deNardo and Grewal 2003; Gupta and Siddiqui 1999; Rovesti et al. 1990). Probably the biggest mistake people make when considering nematodes is assuming that they'll work on insects that aren't in the soil. Unfortunately, these little worms are truly effective only against insects that spend some portion of their life in the ground. One benefit of using nematodes for insects living in the soil is that they'll reproduce themselves and thus will last a lot longer than insecticides.

BENEFITS Under the right conditions these little killers can have a very significant impact on insect pests that live in the soil. Because nematodes reproduce in the body of their host, they can last in the soil for years, providing some level of ongoing control. Nematodes are more compatible with insecticides than most other biological controls.

DRAWBACKS Nematodes don't kill all of an insect population, nor are they particularly effective when weather conditions aren't conducive to their activity. Finally, some people expect these critters to kill non–soil-dwelling insects. While nematodes can kill insects that aren't in the soil, they're much more effective when their targets are living in the ground.

THE BOTTOM LINE Under warm and moist conditions, nematodes are very effective at helping to control soil-dwelling insects for a few years. It's a nice bonus that they're resilient enough to handle some insecticide use, unlike most beneficial insects.

Parasitic wasps

The parasitic wasp you're most likely to buy is the greenhouse whitefly parasite *Encarsia formosa*. This tiny wasp lays eggs inside immature whiteflies that hatch into larvae that eat the young whitefly from the inside out. These wasps are incredibly effective in enclosed spaces, such as greenhouses, but are less effective outside as wind will blow them away from the area where you released them. The biggest problem with these insects is their host range: they'll control whiteflies but nothing else. The aphid parasite *Aphidius colemani* is effective against many aphids but has the same problems as the whitefly parasite in that it will only attack the insect it was released for and it can to be blown to other areas if it's released outdoors. The *Trichogramma* wasp is another popular parasitic wasp that attacks the eggs of various pests, mostly caterpillars, and that has been effective at reducing pest populations. Beneficial wasps don't attack humans and are usually mistaken for insects other than wasps by the casual observer because of their small size.

BENEFITS These wasps tend to be extremely effective at controlling the insect they're released for under ideal circumstances. Since the process of killing the pests actually results in the birth of more wasps, this control can last for a significant amount of time.

DRAWBACKS Parasitic wasps can be blown away by the wind in an outdoor environment and are only useful against one or perhaps a few pests. Parasitic wasps don't kill their host insects quickly, and it's a little bothersome to consider the fact that you've released into the world a small and fearsome parasite that will eat a living being from the inside out.

THE BOTTOM LINE Parasitic wasps work very well in greenhouses where they can find their prey and not be blown away and where the pest to be controlled is usually very well defined. In an outdoor environment these wasps can still work but are somewhat less effective because they may be blown by the wind to other locations.

Predatory mites

You can purchase predatory mites such as *Phytoseiulus persimilis* and *Metaseiulus occidentalis* that will feed on pest mites such as the two-spotted spider mite and the European red mite. Predatory mites can affect other insects, such as thrips and aphids, but the minute pirate bug or big-eyed bug are probably better choices if you want to control a large number of pests. These mites are so tiny that a hand lens is usually necessary to see them. When you do see them they're a blast to watch, because unlike plant-eating mites they move around very quickly like little racecars until they find their prey. These mites are extremely valuable predators, but make sure that it's indeed mites that are the problem before you send in predatory mites. I tend to prefer the minute pirate bug and the big-eyed bug simply because I usually have more problems than just spider mites on my plants.

BENEFITS Predatory mites are very effective at controlling other mites.

DRAWBACKS These mites only attack a few different pests.

 THE BOTTOM LINE If mites are a major problem for you, applying predatory mites makes a lot of sense. If, however, you have multiple types of problem pests, predatory mites probably aren't the way to go.

Organic insecticides

There's a lot of poison out there. This poison can work for us, but it can also work against us. If you're using a chemical to control insect pests in your garden, you need to balance the benefits of using that poison against the potential damage it could cause to both you and the environment in and around your garden. Some groups will tell you that pesticides are completely safe if used according to the label. Wrong. Pesticides are *never* completely safe. What these people should say is that pesticides, when used according to the label, have dangers that would be acceptable to most people who come into contact with them. Of course, there are also people who will tell you that all pesticides are deadly cancer-causing mixtures created by the devil himself. Wrong. Pesticides, if used properly, help us to provide healthy food for ourselves and the world, not to mention controlling diseases such as malaria and yellow fever. I would caution you, as you think about where your opinion lies on the pesticide continuum, to avoid resting at either extreme. My heartfelt opinion is that neither of these positions is adequately supported by the facts. Rather, do some research and spend some time working to figure out where your comfort zone is and then make pesticide choices in your garden from an educated, rather than a reactionary, standpoint.

Before we progress through the insecticides let me make one thing crystal clear. I'm in no way recommending any pesticide, organic or synthetic, for any problem. It's up to you, the consumer, to look at the label of the pesticide that you intend to purchase in order to decide whether that pesticide is appropriate for you. The information I offer can provide some insight into the chemicals you'll see on the active ingredient portion of a pesticide label and nothing more. The label will provide information on the dangers of the pesticide, what problems the pesticide will help to cure, and even which plants the pesticide should and shouldn't be used on. The pesticide label is the law. Don't make applications that are in any way contrary to the label.

OK, so you consider yourself an organic gardener and you normally wouldn't think about using any pesticide, but you've got a terrible insect problem and you've tried everything else. So now you think it's time to pull out the big guns, the insecticides, but you're a little scared of pesticides in general because, after all, they're poisons and could no doubt be detrimental to your health. You decide that organic pesticides are the way to go because they're natural—and thus they must be pretty safe, right? Well, maybe or maybe not. That's what this section is all about.

In the not-so-distant past, organic growers had the option of using any natural insecticide they wanted to. Organic gardeners still have that option today, but truly some of the old natural pesticides can only be called scary. Insecticides like nicotine sulfate were once used on organically grown crops and are now banned for almost all uses by the EPA. I'm sure some gardeners somewhere are still using this insecticide, but I just hope they don't live near me.

Organic insecticides are, in my opinion, one of the worst things ever to happen to the concept of organic growing and gardening. It's not because they're necessarily more or less toxic than synthetic pesticides; they're usually less toxic. The problem is that the public has a perception that because something is organic it's necessarily safe. Despite the constant insistence of people who work with and study pesticides that "organic" doesn't mean "safe," gardeners continue to believe that they're somehow doing something good by applying organic pesticides. I'm frequently assailed by gardeners who seem to regard their use of these poisons as proof that they're saving themselves and the world from synthetic chemicals and certain doom. With gardeners such as these I invariably revert to my snake venom example—I ask them whether snake venom, since it comes from a natural source, would be safer for them than, say, synthetically produced food preservatives. The snake venom is natural, right? It must be safe, right? Wrong. Hey, there's a popular organic pesticide out there that's been used in lab studies to cause Parkinson's disease–like symptoms in rodents. Wanna take a chance that you won't pick it up next time you're at the local garden center? I didn't think so. Nature produces some pretty nasty poisons and carcinogens that can really mess a person up, and everything that comes out of a laboratory isn't necessarily bad. In fact, a lot of synthetic chemicals, commonly known as drugs, are keeping a lot of organic growers alive today.

While I'm wary of organic pesticides, I don't dismiss their usefulness out of hand. Among the pesticides currently in use today, as a group organic pesticides do seem to be somewhat safer than synthetic. But be aware that whenever you use a pesticide, it's wise to check all of the information available about it rather than just assuming that your chances of finding a safe pesticide are better if you choose organic poisons rather than synthetic.

A large number of different insecticides are available for use by the organic grower. These insecticides are widely variable in terms of their efficacy against target pests, toxicity to humans and animals, residual activity, availability in the marketplace, and other properties. Because of these differences, we'll examine commonly used organic insecticides individually instead of looking at them as a group.

Bacillus popilliae

Bacteria that infect and kill insects are attractive because of their specificity to the insect that you're trying to kill. Generally, insecticides that use bacteria as their primary killing agent are considered safe to humans and to insects besides those targeted. *Bacillus popilliae* is more commonly known as milky disease (sometimes this disease is also called milky spore disease, but that's really a trade name for a commercial pesticide) and primarily affects Japanese beetles, though other ground-dwelling insects can be infected. This disease was first identified in the 1940s, though it had been observed infesting Japanese beetles as early as the 1920s. The Japanese beetle came, of course, from Japan and arrived in this country around 1916. Most people assume that *Bacillus popilliae* comes from the East as well, but that's not the case at all. This bacterium was actually first seen in the United States and was not identified in Asia until relatively recently.

Despite a great deal of hullabaloo over the years that this bacterium is an effective agent for controlling the Japanese beetle, it's failed more often than it's succeeded. Some scientists believe that over time, as the Japanese beetle is exposed to this disease more and more, it's becoming less and less effective. In fact, studies conducted in Kentucky in the 1990s showed that commercially available formulations of milky disease were not effective at controlling the Japanese beetle (Redmond and Potter 1995). This disease has been most effective where it's been applied on a regional or statewide basis. Applied to small areas, such as a single garden or even neighborhood, this bacteria is unlikely to provide much control (Weeden et al. 2006).

BENEFITS *Bacillus popilliae* will attack and kill some Japanese beetles. Since it's a living organism, any beetles that are affected will spread the disease when they die and the bacteria can remain in an area for years.

DRAWBACKS This bacterium is most effective when applied to a large area, not just a yard. *Bacillus popilliae* doesn't seem to be as effective as it once was and was never known as a disease that could wipe out a population of Japanese beetles but rather as a way to reduce their numbers.

THE BOTTOM LINE This disease isn't a bad idea for a municipality to apply, but for the typical homeowner it just isn't going to do enough to justify the expense.

Bacillus thuringiensis

Bacillus thuringiensis is my favorite pesticide of all time. It's brewed from a soil-dwelling bacterium that owes its toxicity to a protein commonly referred to as Bt. This protein is so effective that the genes that code for it have been extracted by humans and placed into corn and other plants in order to help those plants defend themselves against caterpillars.

Bacillus thuringiensis was discovered by a Japanese gentleman named S. Ishiwata in 1901 and was incorporated into an insecticidal spray by the French around 1938. This pesticide is a stomach poison and thus needs to be eaten by the insect before it has any effect. After insects feed on the Bt, their stomach walls slowly dissolve and they basically end up digesting themselves. Bt applied to plants should be expected to retain its insecticidal properties for only three to five days after it's been applied, though it may last longer under cool, shady conditions.

Bt is very target-specific, which means that it doesn't generally affect organisms that it's not intended for. Bt products are commonly available for two different types of insects: caterpillars and flies (mosquitoes). A third type of Bt targets beetles and is less commonly available. A Bt that targets caterpillars (*Bacillus thuringiensis kurstaki*) won't affect mosquitoes or beetles; likewise, a Bt that targets mosquitoes (*Bacillus thuringiensis Israelensis*) won't affect caterpillars or beetles, and a Bt that targets beetles (*Bacillus thuringiensis tenebrionis* or *Bacillus thuringinesis* San Diego) won't affect flies or caterpillars. However, when it's repeatedly applied, it may be toxic to certain beneficials such as predatory mites (Papaioannou-Souliotis et al. 1998), although it's likely that this toxicity has more to do with the soaps and oils the Bt is mixed with than the Bt itself. This insecticide has an EIQ of 7.9.

BENEFITS Bt is a very safe insecticide (relatively speaking) that's unlikely to have much effect beyond that intended by the applicator. It's also one of the few insecticides that can be applied without decimating beneficial insect populations. This pesticide stops insects from feeding very rapidly, though it tends to take a long time for the insect to actually die.

DRAWBACKS Bt needs to be eaten by the target insect to have an effect, so good coverage is needed when this pesticide is applied (in other words, try to hit all of the leaves you want to protect). If good coverage isn't obtained, many insects will likely escape by feeding on a leaf or a portion of a leaf that was left untreated. Bt doesn't kill insects quickly, and caterpillars that are poisoned will hang around on the plant where they ingested the Bt, sometimes for a week or more. These caterpillars become emaciated and sickly looking and may hang off of plants in some rather morbid poses. Though the Bt that targets flies is very effective, it works only on mosquito larvae and not on adult mosquitos.

 When used properly Bt is one of the best organic insecticides out there.

Beauvaria bassiana

Ever had athlete's foot so bad you wondered if it could be terminal? For humans it's pretty unlikely, but for insects there's a fungus you can buy that will lead to their demise. This fungus is called *Beauvaria bassiana* and has been sold as Naturalis H&G in the past. It's not easy to find, but it's an effective control for pests such as aphids, thrips, mites, caterpillars, and more. This fungus likes its environment moist and will function best in humid locations. It will last for three to five days in the environment and will also take three to five days to kill pests. This is considered a very safe insecticide.

BENEFITS You get to say that you gave your insect pests a terminal case of athlete's foot!

DRAWBACKS This pesticide is currently hard to find, is not fast acting, and tends not to kill whole populations of insects.

BOTTOM LINE Under wet, humid conditions this is a fantastic insecticide that kills too slowly for most people's tastes, which accounts for the fact that it's so tough to find.

Boric acid

Commonly recommended but absent from the shelves of many garden stores, boric acid can be a useful pesticide affecting many crawling insects. Sold as a powder, or more commonly as the poisonous bait component of ant or cockroach traps, this insecticide works by abrading the insect's exoskeleton and causing the insect to desiccate. Boric acid is also a stomach poison if it's ingested. This poison kills slowly and is usually considered less effective than other commercial insecticides.

Boric acid is one of the safer insecticides if used following label recommendations. This is especially true as it's commonly used in baits and traps, which don't involve spraying and confine the pesticide to a relatively small area that's usually out of the way of most human traffic.

 Boric acid can be reasonably effective against many insects and is relatively safe for humans if used in accordance with the label, though it can have some very negative effects if it's inhaled or ingested.

 This poison doesn't kill quickly, nor is it incredibly effective, with many more insects avoiding death than you might think reasonable.

 This isn't an amazingly effective poison but is a useful constituent in many insect traps. If your expectations for this compound are reasonable, you won't be disappointed. Do expect to wait for some time, perhaps a week or more, before you see a real reduction in pest numbers.

Capsaicin

Hot peppers, which contain the chemical capsaicin, have been used against insects for a long time, but commercially available capsaicin sprays are relatively new. I'm truly comfortable with only a few pesticides in terms of safety, and this is one of them. I'm not saying that pesticides that use capsaicin are perfectly safe. If you've ever touched your eyes after holding or cutting hot peppers, you know that it stings and burns, and at a high enough concentration it may even cause permanent damage. In fact, in some cases hot peppers will even irritate skin, but because buffalo wings are among my favorite foods, when I spray capsaicin I don't feel like I'm exposing my body to anything I wouldn't be exposing it to anyway. Not everyone, of course, is completely sold on the safety of capsaicin. Indeed, some research implies that capsaicin is carcinogenic (Archer and Jones

2002), but this carcinogenicity, if it's indeed real, is most likely realized only with large and repeated doses of capsaicin in the diet. (I wonder if eating buffalo wings every Sunday during the fall counts?)

Using hot peppers for insect control was first reported in 1833, when Dr. William Kenrick recommended syringing a cayenne pepper solution onto plants to kill aphids. Today, hot pepper sprays for insects include capsaicin and usually some sort of wax or oil as well that helps hold this chemical onto the plant so that it will be ready and available when the insect tries to feed. This wax or oil will be detrimental to any insect that it comes into contact with and may even be more effective than the capsaicin itself at killing insects in some circumstances. Capsaicin doesn't work as a poison, at least not at the concentrations typically applied to plants, but rather by repelling insects that don't like its taste. Commercial formulations of capsaicin have been shown to repel insects, including mites and whiteflies, for up to two months (Madanlar et al. 2002), which is quite remarkable compared to many standard pesticides.

BENEFITS If you like hot peppers, hot sauces, or buffalo wings, applying this compound won't subject you to anything you wouldn't be subjected to anyway. A wide variety of insects, including mites, whiteflies, aphids, and mealybugs, will be repelled for a considerable period of time. As a repellent, this compound won't usually have a serious effect on beneficial insects.

DRAWBACKS As a repellent rather than a poison, this compound won't kill insects, so if you spray some plants but not others (or some leaves but not others), insects will simply leave the plants or leaves that have been sprayed in favor of the unsprayed ones. This compound won't be 100 percent effective under most circumstances, so don't expect all of the "bad guys" to just up and disappear. Capsaicin can be formulated as a spray to repel humans and can be extremely irritating, so it must be used with caution. There is some evidence, quickly dismissed by those of us who love Tabasco, that capsaicin is a carcinogen.

THE BOTTOM LINE Capsaicin is an insect repellent that's effective enough for most situations, but it displaces insects rather than actually killing them. This is a good option for those gardeners who aren't ready to use more toxic compounds and who are willing to put up with a little more insect damage to avoid them. I like this stuff.

Citrus oil

Using citrus oils to kill pests is a relatively new idea that originated in the 1980s when researcher Craig Sheppard at the University of Georgia discovered that orange soap would repel ants. The two compounds in citrus oil that are particularly effective against insects are limonene and linalool, both of which act as nerve toxins in insects. One of the problems with citrus oil sprays, though, is that they can be damaging to plant material (Ibrahim et al. 2001). These products tend to be applied at a concentration of from 1 percent to as much as 6 percent citrus oil, which is pretty high for most insecticides and certainly higher than you can achieve with homemade citrus sprays that some people offer recipes for.

If you're particularly concerned about fire ants, you'll be happy to know that a set of trials in Texas has shown that commercial citrus oils can be quite effective at controlling these pests (Brown and Drees 2002). Though usually considered relatively safe, pesticides containing these oils can be skin and eye irritants. An application of a product with citrus oil may last for as long as a few weeks.

BENEFITS Citrus oils are considered to be relatively safe, though they certainly could injure eyes under the right circumstances.

DRAWBACKS I'm always a little frightened when I see products like this, because while they're safe compared to other products, they're not benign. Every pesticide has dangers associated with it. Don't take this one for granted just because it's made with citrus oil. Additionally, this product can damage plants.

 THE BOTTOM LINE Though not for use on plants, citrus oils make sense in many situations because of the safety factor. They're good products to try on ants and ant mounds in particular.

Cryolite (sodium fluoaluminate)

This naturally occurring mineral can be found in various places around the world, including Greenland, though the lion's share of this mineral was used up from this location in the late 1980s. Cryolite has been used as an insecticide since the late 1950s and is effective on a variety of insect pests, including many beetles such as the Colorado potato beetle and many caterpillars that chew on leaves. This pesticide is much less effective on pests that don't chew, such as mites and aphids, because it needs to be ingested by the insect in order for it to work. Cryolite has an EIQ of 21.4 and is not currently allowed for organic production.

Two of the weaknesses of this compound are that it's less effective if it rains much and it loses its efficacy a relatively short time after it's applied, perhaps only a few days (Huang, Smilowitz, and Saunders 1995). Despite this, cryolite residues on crops can reach levels that are unacceptable if about thirty days aren't allowed between application and harvest (Archer and Gauer 1979). This pesticide contains fluoride, and fluoride levels in foods made from treated crops, particularly wines made from treated grapes, do tend to be higher than if the product were not applied (Ostrom 1994). This chemical isn't commonly seen on garden center shelves.

BENEFITS This pesticide is effective against many different chewing insects such as caterpillars and beetles.

DRAWBACKS Fluoride has some toxicity issues that may create a problem if this product is misused.

THE BOTTOM LINE This can be a good product, but care must be taken to ensure that as little as possible of this product is present on foods. This isn't a great choice for most homeowners, even if you can find it, because of the fluoride issue.

Diatomaceous earth

Besides boric acid, another pesticide that's valuable against crawling pests is diatomaceous earth. This is nothing more than the skeletons of long-dead microscopic organisms called diatoms. So how, you're asking yourself, can skeletons control insects? Diatom skeletons aren't made of regular bone; rather, they're made of silicon dioxide, more commonly known as glass. As you probably know, even if you haven't watched Bruce Willis's feet as he walks across crushed glass in the movie *Die Hard*, glass can be quite damaging to living creatures. Fortunately for us, diatom skeletons are so small that they're unlikely to hurt humans unless they're inhaled, in which case the lungs can be injured. The same isn't true of insects; the outer layer of their bodies, called the cuticle, can be badly abraded by contact with this stuff if they crawl across a line of it. Since insects rely on this cuticle to retain their internal moisture levels, damage results in desiccation and eventual death.

 Diatomaceous earth is relatively safe as long as it isn't inhaled and can be quite effective at deterring and killing pests under appropriate conditions. Additionally, it gave me the opportunity to talk about one of my favorite works of fiction, *Die Hard*.

 Diatomaceous earth can be dangerous if inhaled, and it loses some of its effectiveness when it gets wet. This product won't kill insects quickly.

BOTTOM LINE This is a great product if used properly.

Garlic

Commercial insecticides made out of garlic are becoming more popular, and though I rarely see them in garden centers, they can be found all over the Web. Garlic-based pesticides are known to be both poisonous and repellent to various insects. The active ingredients in sprays made with garlic include the chemicals diallyl disulfide and diallyl trisulfide. Garlic insecticides are usually made of a mixture of the essential oil of garlic and water. You can make these sprays in a homemade concoction that may be even more effective than the commercial products, but more potentially dangerous for you as well. Homemade sprays can be made by mixing about four and a half ounces of garlic extract with a few drops of some type of soap in about a quart of water and then blending and straining the resulting mixture. Mixtures similar to this one have been shown to be more effective than commercial garlic sprays in some research (Flint et al. 1995).

Garlic sprays were first shown to be effective against ticks in the 1950s and today these sprays are known to have effects against many insects, including whiteflies, aphids, and beetles (Flint et al. 1995; Hori 1996; Huang, Chen, and Ho 2000). Garlic isn't known to be particularly toxic to humans, but it can be irritating to skin and eyes at the high concentrations found in commercial products.

BENEFITS This is certainly one of the safer insect sprays you can buy or even make. It has proven to be effective against a wide range of insects.

DRAWBACKS Since garlic acts primarily as a repellent, it won't kill most of the pests that you might like dead. It's important to be sure that every leaf you want to protect gets a shot of the stuff. Garlic sprays may cause some leaf burn so need to be tested on plants and not just applied willy-nilly.

THE BOTTOM LINE I like garlic a lot. It has proven to be reasonably effective and is safer than many other insecticides that you could choose.

Hellebore

Hellebore comes from the plants *Veratrum viride* (American hellebore) and *V. album* (white hellebore). This pesticide was once a standard in insect control but is now rarely seen, though I've heard of some people mixing it up for themselves. The plants from which the pesticide are derived can be found growing wild in the United States; however, real concerns about the toxicity of this plant make it less than attractive as an alternative to synthetic pesticides. For example, a closely related species that contains many of the same chemicals, *V. californicum*, has been known to cause serious facial deformities, such as the presence of only a single central eye (cyclopsia), in lambs born to sheep that ingest this plant. In fact, in the mid-1900s up to 25 percent of pregnant sheep that fed in the hills of Idaho had lambs that were affected (James et al. 2004). Hellebore contains several alkaloids that are known to be toxic to insects and that can also be quite toxic to humans. I've never actually seen this insecticide available for sale, though it isn't all that difficult to find the plants that produce this poison.

In the early 1900s, when hellebore was commonly used as an insecticide, it was applied at relatively high concentrations, greater than what most of today's pesticides require. Though once a useful pesticide, this killer was supplanted even before DDT came onto the scene in the 1940s by such compounds as lead and calcium arsenate.

 Hellebore is toxic to many insects.

 The requirement for relatively high concentrations to kill insects and major concerns about the safety of this compound make me doubtful about the wisdom of using it.

 Marginal efficacy and concerns about toxicity problems make this a pesticide to avoid.

Kaolin

Though most pesticides work by poisoning insects, some work by creating a physical barrier around the plant that requires protection. One such pesticide is kaolin, usually sold as Surround. This product is nothing more than a form of clay, composed primarily of silicon and aluminum, that's mined mostly in the state of Georgia. This product is also used in the food industry to prevent caking.

Kaolin has been shown to be effective at inhibiting attacks from a number of pests, including codling moths and aphids attacking apple trees (Burgel, Daniel, and Wyss 2005; Unruh et al. 2000). Applications of kaolin need to be made quite regularly for this product to work, as it will wash off, and in general this product doesn't seem to be as effective as other commercial insecticides. Additionally, this product is reflective, resulting in a whitish hue on treated trees. Beneficial insects aren't generally harmed by application of this clay. The EIQ for this product is 8.

 This is a relatively safe compound (you've got to like any compound with an EIQ of only 8) that has proven to be reasonably effective at controlling many insects, particularly those affecting fruit trees, when properly applied.

DRAWBACKS This product needs to be reapplied frequently and isn't considered to be quite as effective as poison-based insecticides.

THE BOTTOM LINE If you're willing to reapply this product relatively frequently (following label instructions), it has good potential for helping to reduce populations of pest insects.

Neem

This is the "greatest pesticide ever" according to some organic producers. Neem, also known as azidirachtin, comes from the tropical tree *Azadirachta indica*. This insecticide has become very popular recently because of its lack of toxicity to animals and its ability to help control fungi as well as insects.

Neem works on insects in two ways. First, it acts as a growth regulator, meaning that it prevents insects from developing properly (they can't molt from one life stage into the next), and second, it acts to stop the insect from feeding. Neem is effective against aphids, many caterpillars and beetles, and a host of other pests. An application of a pesticide that has neem as its active ingredient should last about a week.

Most people who apply neem will apply it in very small doses that shouldn't be toxic to people or animals. However, allergies to neem have been reported, as have negative effects on sperm and abortive effects in rats, and aflatoxin (an extremely potent natural carcinogen) may be present in neem if it's not properly treated during processing (Boeke et al. 2004). Despite these concerns, Boeke et al. conclude that "if applied with care the use of especially unprocessed and aqueous neem-based products should not be discouraged." Besides having human health issues, neem is also toxic to many aquatic organisms, so it should be used with care around bodies of water. Neem has a surprisingly low EIQ of 12.8.

Besides its activity against insects, neem can also be used as a fungicide. Neem's claim to fame is its excellent efficacy against powdery mildew. It will also be effective against a range of other diseases such as leaf spots. Unfortunately, neem tends to be ineffective against black spot on roses (McGovern et al. 2003; Mulrooney 2003).

BENEFITS Used at recommended doses and with care, neem is considered a relatively safe insecticide that does work well against a wide variety of pests, including some diseases.

DRAWBACKS Some findings indicate that if misused or used improperly, this pesticide could have significant adverse effects on humans and the environment.

THE BOTTOM LINE Neem is a useful tool for the grower who wants to employ organic insecticides, but a few question marks about the safety of this compound make me somewhat hesitant about using it despite its low EIQ.

Nicotine

Nicotine, including tobacco leaves, really shouldn't be on this list because it has been banned for most uses, including all commercial organic growing. Nonetheless, it's still sometimes used by growers and gardeners who think that because tobacco is a plant anything that comes from it must be safe. This is, of course, a ridiculous assumption, especially considering the amount of lung cancer in the world. Nicotine is extremely toxic and has little place in organic or conventional production because it's so poisonous. In fact, nicotine sulfate used to be one of the most toxic pesticides that we used, ranking very close to the synthetic pesticide aldicarb (which we'll discuss later). Nicotine is a nerve toxin that acts very quickly and is very dangerous to a wide variety of animals.

BENEFITS This stuff will kill pests very quickly and efficiently.

DRAWBACKS It's just too darn dangerous.

THE BOTTOM LINE Don't use this pesticide.

Oils

One of the most useful of the organic sprays is oil. Oil works as an insecticide by surrounding and suffocating the target insect. Insects breathe through little holes along the sides of their bodies, called spiracles. If these spiracles are blocked, the insect runs into problems and eventually dies. Though oils are usually listed as acceptable for organic growers to use, they're often synthetically produced. There are both summer and dormant oils. Dormant oils, usually applied in the winter, are thicker and more effective than summer oils but also more dangerous for leaves, so can only be applied when leaves aren't present. Summer oils, on the other hand, are lighter and are less likely to damage foliage; they're useful against many insects, most notably aphids, scale, and mites. Unfortunately, even summer sprays do have limitations and may still damage foliage. Dormant oil sprays are one of the best defenses against insects that we have. They kill pests while they're trying to ride out the winter, giving the tree a head start in the spring. The EIQ of horticultural oils is 27.5, which may seem a little high for something that's supposed to be low risk, but beneficial insects and plants can be hurt by oil applications.

BENEFITS If used properly, oils are relatively safe pesticides that can be quite effective.

DRAWBACKS Oils can burn leaves. Even the very fine oils can cause problems under extreme conditions. Oils rarely completely control a population of insect pests and can kill beneficial insects.

THE BOTTOM LINE Oils are a good idea, but be careful to use them properly and in accordance with label instructions. I particularly like using oils when a plant is dormant. It gives the plant a good head start in the spring by knocking out problems before they arise.

Pyrethrum

The most commonly used organic pesticide, pyrethrum, comes from a species of chrysanthemum, *Chrysanthemum cinerariaefolium*, grown primarily in Africa; this plant may also be found in other areas such as Australia, and at least one researcher, Dr. Jeanine Davis, has looked into trying to grow this plant for production in the United States. Pyrethrum flowers have been known as a folk insecticide for many years, with the practice originating in Persia (Iran) and then moving into Dalmatia (Croatia), where the commercial pyrethrum industry started in the 1840s (Nelson 1975). Pyrethrum is actually a combination of many different chemicals, such as pyrethrin and cinerin, rather than a single one. Some of these chemicals can be produced synthetically instead of harvested, and you'll often see commercial pesticides on garden center shelves that contain synthetic forms of these naturally occurring products. Since the chemicals that make up pyrethrum have somewhat similar properties, it's easiest to treat pyrethrum as a single compound.

Pyrethrum acts in a way that's very similar to many of the synthetic pesticides. It affects the transmission of nerve impulses to and from the brain. This would seem to make it a pretty dangerous compound for humans, except that humans have an enzyme that detoxifies it before it reaches the nerves where it can do damage. That doesn't mean that this compound is safe, though, and it should be considered dangerous by anyone using it. Though pyrethrum can be used alone, it's often mixed with piperonyl butoxide (which is derived from safrole, a once-common natural flavoring from the sassafras tree that's now banned from food because it has been shown to be mildly carcinogenic) or in some cases with sesame oil, to increase its effectiveness.

This insecticide is a common choice for wasp sprays because it acts so quickly to disrupt insects' nerve impulses, knocking them right out of the sky. This is certainly something that those who've ever been chased by a wasp can appreciate. Besides wasp sprays pyrethrum is also used in a number of other types of insecticidal sprays, such as those used for aphids, whiteflies, and scale. Pyrethrum has been used enough that there's resistance to it among some insects. It's degraded by sunlight, so the more sun it's exposed to after it's sprayed the more quickly it will break down. You shouldn't expect it to last for longer than a day under most circumstances, and it usually lasts for a shorter time than that. The EIQ of pyrethrum is around 18; the EIQ of piperonyl butoxide is 20.8.

BENEFITS   Pyrethrum is extremely fast acting and very effective. Because this compound breaks down so rapidly, it's only present in the area where it's applied for a very short period of time.

DRAWBACKS This poison breaks down rapidly so is only toxic for a very short time. It's very toxic to beneficial insects as well as pests, and some pests may have some resistance to it.

THE BOTTOM LINE Used properly, this is an excellent "knock down" pesticide because it works rapidly to kill insects by messing up their nervous systems. This pesticide is often considered safe by gardeners, but it's not completely safe and should be used with the same respect afforded to any potent poison.

Quassia

Here's an almost unlocatable organic pesticide that's always listed in organic gardening books. Quassia is derived from the bark of various plants, including *Quassia amara* and *Picrasma excelsa*. This insecticide works primarily as a stomach toxin so needs to be ingested by the insect for it to be most effective, though it has been reported to act as both a contact insecticide and a systemic, which means that it will actually get into the vascular system of the plant and be transported throughout its branches and leaves, thereby providing allover protection (Roark 1947; Stoll 1988).

Although extensive testing hasn't been done on the toxicity of quassia, it's not considered particularly toxic to humans. In fact, historically this compound has been considered as a substitute for hops in beer (Enders 1868) and as a useful remedy for "putrid fevers" and intestinal worms (Lindsay 1794; McIndoo and Sievers 1917; Paarmann 1779), though I personally would stay away from it for these purposes.

Quassia was first recorded as a useful insecticide in 1885 when Eleanor Olmerod mixed six pounds of quassia chips with one hundred gallons of water and three gallons of soft soap and applied it to hop plants to try to get rid of the hops aphid. Since that time this poison has been used successfully against a wide variety of insects such as aphids and many beetles and moths (Stoll 1988). The fumes of burning quassia wood have also been shown to be somewhat effective against mosquitoes (Howard 1900; McIndoo and Sievers 1917).

Though plenty of literature is available demonstrating that quassia is a useful insecticide, it's not frequently used today, probably because it's slow acting and not as effective as many other insecticides that can be purchased for a much lower price.

Quassia can be an effective insecticide and is one of the few botanical insecticides that can act systemically in a plant.

 This is a difficult-to-find insecticide that takes a long time to kill the insects that are treated.

Quassia is tough to find and it isn't as effective as many other insecticides. Additionally, the possible health dangers of this pesticide haven't been researched to the level that I'd like to see, so I would avoid it though it certainly has potential.

Rotenone

My least favorite pesticide is rotenone. It's certainly not the most dangerous pesticide out there, but it's among the most dangerous organic insecticides you can use—and that, coupled with the fact that many people associate "organic" with "safe," creates a bad situation. Rotenone comes from a number of different plants but most commonly from *Derris elliptica* and other plants in this genus. Rotenone has been used for centuries as a fish toxin (McIndoo, Sievers, and Abbott 1919) and is still considered one of the more effective piscicides (fish poisons) available. Rotenone works to kill organisms primarily by respiratory paralysis.

Rotenone has proven to be one of the most effective of the organic insecticides. It rapidly stops insects from feeding and kills them within a day or two of exposure. This poison is also notable in that it breaks down relatively quickly in sunlight and is viable for only two or three days after it's applied. All of this makes rotenone sound pretty benign, but that's really the furthest thing from the truth. Besides its acute toxicity, rotenone has been found to cause Parkinson's disease–like symptoms when injected just below the skin of rats at extremely low doses (Caboni et al. 2004). I consider rotenone's EIQ of only 33 to be quite misleading.

Rotenone's ability to kill aquatic life makes this pesticide incredibly dangerous to apply near bodies of water. It's always stunning to me when I go to a Web site selling organic products and see it refer to studies that have shown that commercial formulations of glyphosate can be toxic to frogs as proof of the environmental hazards of using synthetic chemicals and then, sometimes on the same page, advertise an insecticide using rotenone. You can call this what you will; I call it hypocrisy.

 Rotenone is a potent poison for insects.

DRAWBACKS This compound is dangerous to beneficial insects and fish, and is more toxic to humans than most other pesticides, organic or synthetic. Although there's no known link between this pesticide and Parkinson's disease in humans, the fact that it causes symptoms similar to this disease in rats worries me.

THE BOTTOM LINE Why would any sane person use this pesticide?

Ryania

There are five or six well-known organic insecticides that are named as effective by almost every organic resource I know of but almost impossible to find reliably. The reason for this is usually that the formulator of the pesticide has decided to withdraw it from the market, most often because it just doesn't make enough money for them. Ryania is one of these insecticides. Ryania has been used since the late 1920s to control various insects, most notably sugarcane and corn borers. This compound comes from the ground-up stems of the South American shrub *Ryania speciosa* and kills insects by causing nerve impulses that lead to sustained contraction of muscles and eventually death. Not much information is available about ryania's toxicity beyond some very basic data. Ryania is considered slightly toxic to humans and is toxic to birds, bees, and beneficial insects, which results in its EIQ of 55.3.

BENEFITS Ryania is effective against a broad spectrum of insects.

DRAWBACKS This compound is tough to find and information on its safety is spotty.

This product is tough to find for a reason. There are other products that are more thoroughly tested and more effective.

Sabadilla

Almost every organic gardening book I pick up has sabadilla listed as an organic insecticide that's easy to find and useful for keeping insect pests at bay. Sabadilla will certainly keep pests at bay, and a huge body of literature describes its effectiveness against a wide variety of insects, but this stuff isn't easy to find. In fact, even on the Internet where stuff like this is usually readily available, I've had a tremendously difficult time finding it for sale, which is almost certainly because the manufacturer voluntarily decided to stop manufacturing this chemical.

Sabadilla comes from various species in the genus *Schoenocaulon*, which is a sort of lily. This insecticide was used most in the 1940s and 1950s but was never a really popular choice. It's reported to have been used to control vermin and lice as far back as the 1500s (Griffith 1847; Zornig 1909).

Sabadilla is primarily considered a stomach poison, indicating that an insect must ingest it in order for it to work effectively. But some tests have shown it to be effective as a contact poison as well (Allen, Dicke, and Harris 1944), meaning that insects that simply come into contact with it will be adversely affected. In terms of its toxicity, sabadilla is considered to be one of the more toxic organic insecticides for humans. It's also toxic to beneficial insects and has an EIQ of 35.6.

 Sabidilla can be an effective insecticide when used properly and has a longer residual than most other organic pesticides.

 The biggest problems with sabadilla are that it's tremendously difficult to find, it's not as effective as many other pesticides, and it's more dangerous to humans than many other insecticides.

 Better choices are available in terms of both effectiveness and safety, so it's no wonder that this particular insecticide is hard to find.

Soaps

Soap is one of the oldest insecticides available for use by homeowners. These compounds have been used for years, and though many soaps aren't completely organic but are created from synthetic chemicals, they're still widely accepted by organic gardeners and growers alike as a natural, or at least safe, product. Soaps work to control insects by removing their waxy cuticle, causing them to desiccate and die. These chemicals don't work quickly but they do tend to work well, especially against soft-bodied insects such as aphids and mealybugs.

Insecticidal soaps have an EIQ of about 19. Though soaps are generally considered safe for humans and the environment, they can hurt soft-bodied beneficial insects and aquatic creatures. Also keep in mind that the more effective a soap is at getting rid of insects, the more effective it will be at taking the cuticle off of plants. Plants that have strong soaps applied to them may be damaged. Commercial insecticidal soaps are usually pretty safe for plants if label instructions are followed, but homemade soap mixtures should be tested on a small portion of the plant that might be damaged before they're applied to the entire plant.

 Soaps are relatively safe for humans and can be effective against many soft-bodied pests.

 Soaps aren't completely safe, especially for plants, so care needs to be taken when applying these sprays.

 Soaps are a great choice for insect problems when the problem is an aphid or a mite. These sprays are safer for humans than most other choices and can be quite effective.

Spinosad

A newer organic insecticide that has a great deal of potential is spinosad, which comes from *Saccharopolyspora spinosa*, a soil-dwelling fungus. This toxin works by affecting the insect's nervous system, but unlike many other insecticides that attack the nervous system, this product tends to work slowly. Although it acts quickly to stop insects from feeding, it may take a few days to kill them. Spinosad is supposed to be particularly effective against caterpillars, flies, and thrips, and may be effective against some beetles and grasshoppers but isn't useful for controlling sucking insects such as aphids or stinkbugs (Thompson, Hutchins, and Sparks 1999). Spinosad can be effective against pests for as long as four weeks after it's applied.

This compound is a particularly attractive product because it has very low toxicity to nontarget insects and people, and thus far tests of its carcinogenicity have shown it to be noncarcinogenic. It's considered to be safer for beneficial insects than most other organic and synthetic pesticides. It has an EIQ of 17.7 and seems likely to become a pesticide of choice in the near future.

BENEFITS This is one of the best choices available for gardeners with thrip problems. Evidence seems to indicate that this is a relatively safe insecticide for humans. Spinosad has good residual activity.

DRAWBACKS This pesticide kills slowly and is effective only on certain insects, including caterpillars, flies, and thrips.

THE BOTTOM LINE This is a relatively new organic insecticide with a lot of potential, especially for controlling thrips.

Synthetic insecticides

Humans started using insecticides because we were losing too many of our crops to insects. It's as simple as that. If we weren't losing crops why would we use pesticides? They're dangerous and expensive! When we discovered that we could make insecticides that were more effective than the ones we could collect from nature, there was no question that we would do just that. In general, today's synthetic pesticides are more effective than their organic counterparts; however, these synthetic pesticides also tend to be more toxic to humans, more damaging to beneficial insects, and more ecologically disruptive than their organic counterparts. Still, there are ways to minimize the effects of any pesticide on the environment if some time and care are taken.

A huge number of synthetic insecticides are available; most of these insecticides can be classified into groups with those that behave similarly.

These groupings can provide useful generalizations about pesticides, but within a class every pesticide is different and has different abilities to control target pests as well as differing human toxicities and potential environmental effects. I discuss the classes of insecticides you're likely to see, but keep in mind that new insecticides are introduced and made available to homeowners all the time, and insecticides are also lost on a consistent basis as their dangers start to outweigh their usefulness. The insecticides we see on the shelves now aren't necessarily the ones that will be available in the next decade or even the next year.

Abamectin

Abamectin is actually a mixture of chemicals called avermectins that come from a soil bacterium known as *Streptomyces avermitilis*. Though this insecticide is derived from a bacteria, it's not currently allowed for use by commercial organic growers, so I've decided to place it in the synthetics section. Avermectins work to kill insects by affecting the transmission of messages from the brain to the muscles. This pesticide can be absorbed through the leaf surface, meaning that an entire leaf will become toxic to insects despite the fact that the entire leaf wasn't treated. Abamectin isn't considered a true systemic, though, because it's not transferred through plant stem tissue.

Abamectin can control insects for up to thirty days and is particularly effective on mites, leaf miners, and thrips; it may also be quite toxic to beneficial insects. This chemical is highly toxic to aquatic organisms. It's considered moderately toxic to humans if ingested, which basically means that it isn't nearly as safe as something like *Bacillus thuringiensis* or kaolin. Its EIQ is 38.

BENEFITS This is a very effective insecticide for a wide variety of pests including mites, leaf miners, and thrips. It also has a nice long residual, up to a month.

DRAWBACKS This chemical isn't currently considered organic by commercial organic producers. It can be quite toxic to fish and beneficial organisms.

THE BOTTOM LINE This is a good choice for mites, leaf miners, and thrips, but it has some significant drawbacks that need to be considered before using it.

Carbamates

Carbamates were created in the early 1950s and kill insects by disrupting their nerve impulses. As nerve poisons, carbamates tend to be quite toxic to humans as well, just like the organophosphates we'll investigate in an upcoming section. Some carbamates are systemic and are taken up by plants, while others aren't.

One of the better-known and most toxic pesticides ever used was a carbamate by the name of aldicarb. This chemical was great because it could be applied to the roots of a plant and would be rapidly carried up into the canopy of the plant by its vascular system, making every leaf on the plant a toxic treat for insects. It was wonderfully effective on a wide variety of sucking insects such as aphids and scale. Unfortunately, this compound was also taken up by any other plant in the area. Though I'm not sure if it's true, it's been said that if you applied this compound to turf one morning it would be taken up by the grass and by the next morning the dew on the grass would be so toxic that you wouldn't be able to travel a hundred yards barefoot without being poisoned. This is one researcher who's gonna leave that story alone!

But aldicarb isn't the only carbamate insecticide out there; in fact, another chemical in this class, carbaryl, has been extremely useful in the garden since it was introduced in 1956. Carbaryl, also known by the name Sevin, is the carbamate seen most commonly by the gardener. This chemical, unlike aldicarb, isn't taken up by a plant's vascular system. The EIQ of carbaryl is 21.7. Carbaryl has been used on a variety of insect pests but is particularly effective against beetles, especially, and unfortunately, ladybugs. (Some people find it to be very effective against the Asian ladybeetle, which is often considered a nuisance to homes during the winter, though it's also a beneficial insect that eats aphids and other pests.) This insecticide will last about a week after being applied before it breaks down. Because it's been around for so long and used on so many insects, a number of insect pests have developed resistance to carbaryl.

A second, newer carbamate insecticide that's often seen in ant baits is indoxacarb. This compound has an EIQ of 43 when it's applied as a spray. Used as a bait for ants the EIQ should be much lower. A third carbamate with a high EIQ of 87.3 when it's used as a spray is propoxur. This is a very toxic compound that should be avoided when possible. Once again, when used as a bait the danger of this pesticide should be much reduced, which is not to say that the chemical is less poisonous, just that it's less likely to be in a situation where a person, animal, or beneficial insect would be poisoned by it.

 Carbamates can be very effective against many pests. Carbaryl is especially effective against beetles.

 Carbaryl is known as a ladybug killer, for good reason. Some of the other carbamates, besides carbaryl, are extremely toxic.

 Carbamates aren't bad choices if you need to use an insecticide, but these products can be very toxic to beneficial insects and humans, so they need to be used very selectively and carefully.

DDT and other chlorinated hydrocarbons

This group of insecticides started the whole debate about the safety of pesticides and was the primary target of Rachel Carson's ire in *Silent Spring*. The best-known compound in this chemical class is DDT, even though it hasn't been available in the United States for many years. Other chemicals in this class include aldrin, dieldrin, endrin, lindane, chlordane, and a host of others, most of them currently banned for use in most nations. One of the chlorinated hydrocarbons still largely available is methoxychlor (EIQ 53.7), though its time may soon be coming to an end as well.

The chlorinated hydrocarbons primarily affect insects by stopping nerve impulses from shutting off. Though as a nerve toxin you would expect DDT to be very toxic to humans as well, that isn't the case at all. DDT has major environmental problems associated with it, but its toxicity to humans is very low, which is why it was used to control lice and mosquitoes in the 1940s, 1950s, and 1960s. I don't advocate that DDT ever be made available again, but keep in mind that this chemical saved many human lives by helping to control diseases like malaria, typhus, and yellow fever.

One of the weaknesses of the chlorinated hydrocarbons and one of the big reasons that this group of chemicals was taken off the market is that as a group they're so chemically stable. It takes a long time for these chemicals to break down in the environment. Another weakness is that their use was so widespread that many insects became very resistant to them.

 These were, and in some cases still are, effective insect killers.

 These insecticides just last too darn long in the environment, and many insects are now resistant to them.

 The chlorinated hydrocarbons were very important insecticides that came around at a time when we needed them to help control insects that carried disease. They've done their duty and now it's time for us to move on without them. I would say good riddance, but DDT saved billions of people from disease over the years and to dismiss that out of hand would be callous.

Growth regulators

Among the safest insecticides are growth regulators. These chemicals mimic natural insect hormones and cause problems as the insect matures and attempts to molt. While typically made synthetically, they're considered quite safe because they have such a specific mode of action against insects. Some of the more common growth regulators include hydroprene, metheprene, and kinoprene. Perhaps the biggest drawback of these compounds is that they don't provide the quick and satisfying knockdown that the nerve toxins do, but that doesn't make them any less effective at actually killing insects. These chemicals affect growing insects and are not effective against adults. Products containing these chemicals are usually used primarily against cockroaches.

 These chemicals tend to be safer than many other pesticides used for the same thing and are quite effective at controlling certain pests.

These products don't kill insects quickly and are really only available for killing a few insect pests, including cockroaches.

 These are good, relatively safe chemicals that are available for controlling a relatively small number of pests.

Neonicotinoids

A newer synthetic pesticide that's getting and will certainly continue to get a lot of attention is imidacloprid. This is considered a relatively safe insecticide with a relatively low toxicity to humans and an EIQ of 34.9 because of possible environmental effects. It's a systemic and so will move through a plant's vascular system, slaying insects as it goes. It's effective on a wide variety of pests but may harm beneficial insects, such as ladybugs, that feed on the pollen of treated plants (Smith and Krischik 1999), and it doesn't control mites and may even make outbreaks worse (Raupp et al. 2004).

There are two things to like about this insecticide: its residual activity, which may last a month or longer, and the fact that it's one of the few chemicals that the typical tree owner can buy that will really help with borers (insects that get under the bark of certain trees and can cause major problems by interfering with the plant's sap flow). Few other pesticides available to the typical tree owner can really help with these pests. Though imidacloprid is the most common neonicotinoid out there, more will probably be available in the next few years.

 Imidacloprid—and other neonicotinoids as they become available—is of relatively low toxicity to humans and is very useful against many insect pests. This product lasts for a long time after it's applied. Imidacloprid is one of the best products available for use against borers.

Imidacloprid can be present in a plant's pollen and thus be toxic to insects you'd rather not harm, such as ladybugs. This product can actually cause an increase in mite populations, perhaps because of its effects on predatory insects.

THE BOTTOM LINE This is a good product to use if you have problems with borers and certain other insects. This is not a good product to use if you have mites.

Organophosphates

Here's a group of insecticides that come directly from a line of research on chemicals intended to kill humans—how lovely! Research into nerve gasses by the Nazis (and by other nations) in the 1930s and 1940s led to the discovery that some of these compounds affected not only humans but also insects. Further research showed that some of the chemicals that weren't particularly good at killing people were actually quite good at knocking out insects, leading to this class of insecticides. Over the years a number of different organophosphate insecticides have been used in gardens, though many have been taken off of the market due primarily to health concerns. Organophosphates disrupt the nervous system of insects by inhibiting nerve impulses from being shut off. Since humans also have nerves, this class of insecticides can be particularly dangerous to humans, though some are more toxic than others.

Most organophosphate insecticides are poisonous to a wide variety of insects, including both pests and beneficial insects. Organophosphate insecticides tend to have a moderate to long residual, lasting anywhere from a day or two to a month or even a little longer.

A number of organophosphate insecticides may be used by a typical gardener. Perhaps the worst of the organophosphates, at least to the homeowner, is disulfoton, also known as disyston. This insecticide is extremely toxic to humans, which is offset in the mind of many by the fact that it's extremely effective. It's usually sold in granular form. As the granules dissolve this pesticide is taken up by the plant's roots and distributed throughout its tissues. This insecticide is often combined with fertilizer and marketed for roses. Disyston represents about the worst that the organophosphates have to offer, with an incredibly hefty EIQ of 104.

One of more innocuous organophosphate insecticides out there in terms of its effects on humans and the environment is acephate, more commonly known as orthene. Orthene has an EIQ of 23.4 and is effective against insects for a week or longer. A third organophosphate insecticide used commonly by gardeners is malathion. This product has an EIQ of

23.8 and is, along with orthene, among the safer organophosphates. Malathion has a very short residual life and won't affect insects for longer than a few days at most.

Resistance to organophosphates has been observed in many different insects, including whiteflies, mosquitoes, and aphids. When an insecticide has been around as long as the organophosphates, it's no surprise that resistance has developed.

BENEFITS Organophosphates have been around for a long time and have been very effective against many different pests. There are few classes of chemicals with the track record of killing insects that the organophosphates have.

DRAWBACKS Organophosphates, as a group, tend to be pretty toxic, especially if you pick the wrong ones. Increasing insect resistance means that they're becoming less and less effective as time goes on. Organophosphates tend to be toxic to a wide variety of insects, both the bad and the good. Because of these problems, many of the organophosphates that we have now won't be available in the coming years.

THE BOTTOM LINE This is an old class of insecticides that has served its purpose and that for the most part should probably go the way of the dodo, with the possible exception of orthene and one or two others.

Pyrethroids (synthetic pyrethrins)

We've already taken a look at the natural insecticide pyrethrum. This insecticide is fast acting, affects a wide range of different insect pests, and is relatively short lived in the environment. Pyrethroids are basically just synthetic versions of the chemicals in pyrethrum, altered to break down less quickly.

Pyrethroids kill insects very quickly by short-circuiting the transmission of signals along nerves. Some of these chemicals are relatively safe for humans, because we have an enzyme that breaks these toxins down before they can cause too much damage, but some are quite toxic. A number of generations of pyrethroids have been created as insects have become resistant to the older compounds, with each generation providing better residuals, greater efficacy, and in some cases lower toxicity. Of the pyrethroids available today, a few are worth noting because they're so commonly available and so effective.

The pyrethroid most likely to end up in gardeners' hands is permethrin, which has been around since 1974 and is considered a second-generation pyrethroid. Permethrin is available in many different products from a number of companies and is an extremely effective insecticide. It has all of the good characteristics of pyrethrum and breaks down much more slowly because it's not as affected by sunlight as the natural chemicals that make up pyrethrum. Permethrin has been around for long enough that some insects have developed resistance to it, but it's still highly effective against most garden pests. Permethrin has an EIQ of 88. This number is high primarily because of how damaging this chemical can be to beneficial insects such as ladybugs and bees. It can also be quite toxic to aquatic life. This chemical is likely to be effective against insects for a week or two and isn't taken up into the plant's vascular system.

Other pyrethroids that are or might be available to the general consumer in the near future include allethrin (EIQ 36.1), bifenthrin (EIQ 87.8), cyfluthrin (EIQ 39.6), cypermethrin (EIQ 27.3), deltamethrin (EIQ 25.7), esfenvalerate (EIQ 39.6), imiprothrin, lambda-cyhalothrin (EIQ 43.5), resmethrin (EIQ 33.6), sumithrin, and tetramethrin. Most of these have a relatively low toxicity to humans (though eye and skin irritation may be caused by some) but may have effects on the environment similar to permethrin, which accounts for their high EIQs. Additionally, most of these chemicals will continue to kill insects for a week or two after application, with the exception of resmethrin, which tends to break down in a day or two, especially in sunny conditions.

BENEFITS Pyrethroids kill pest insects quickly and are effective on a wide variety of pests. These poisons usually have a good residual, often lasting for a week or two.

DRAWBACKS Some insects are resistant to pyrethroids, and these chemicals, being broad-spectrum killers, are usually very good at killing beneficial insects. They will also kill aquatic life. Some of the pyrethroids can be quite toxic to humans.

These are very effective poisons that kill many different insect pests quickly. If you need something like that, look no further. But be aware that these compounds have significant drawbacks, including killing beneficial insects and aquatic life. For me these chemicals are an option of last resort only.

Other synthetic insecticides

A few other commonly used insecticides don't fit nicely into classes like the ones above and aren't seen commonly enough to devote a full section to. Some of these that you might see include fenbutatin-oxide, a chemical used for killing mites; fipronil (EIQ 90), a nerve poison often used for household insects such as ants; and hydramethylnon, an insecticide often used in cockroach traps.

Practices designed to increase pesticide efficacy

A wide assortment of practices can be followed to reduce how much pesticide needs to be applied to control insect pests. Most people who use pesticides actually use these practices in one form or another whether they realize it or not, just by following their own common sense. If you're the kind of person who's willing to apply insecticides but want to minimize your use of these chemicals, the following are strategies for doing just that.

Trap cropping

Get 'em all in one spot and then blow 'em away! Are there certain plants that more than other plants attract the pests you most worry about? If so, you can treat the pest on those plants (the trap crop) before the pest spreads. A good example of this is the Japanese beetle and roses. Japanese beetles prefer roses to almost any other plant in the garden. If you kill the Japanese beetles when they first start feeding on your roses, you will have prevented some of the damage they might otherwise cause to other plants in the area.

Trap cropping can greatly reduce the use of pesticides and the damage to plants besides the ones used as the trap crop.

The trap crop will suffer, and this technique won't provide 100-percent control of pests.

 This is a useful technique that can really put a hurting on a particular pest. It still employs pesticides and isn't a cure-all, but it's very effective at limiting pesticide use.

Spot spraying

Applying insecticides only where they're needed is underappreciated in the gardening world. Many people see a problem and immediately apply a poison to absolutely everything. This practice has its advantages—you'll definitely kill more pests—but you'll also kill beneficial insects and apply more pesticide that may very well be detrimental to your health. Instead, why not just spray the spots where you see the insects? Sure, it takes more time to figure out where they are, but the reduced pesticide use is worth it.

 You'll reduce pesticide use and effects on beneficial insects.

 You'll need to take the time to figure out where the pests are.

 If you're going to use a poison, there's no reason not to use this technique besides the extra time it takes. This is time well spent.

Chemical rotation

When you use any insecticides, be they organic or synthetic, one of the most important practices to follow is chemical rotation. This is basically nothing more than making sure that you use different chemicals over time to control a particular pest. This is important because if you consistently use the same chemical, you'll end up allowing all of the insects that are resistant to this chemical to survive. As an example, think of a leaf with fifty aphids on it. If you apply a dose of an insecticide to this leaf most of these aphids will die, but probably not all. That's because aphids, like humans, have different susceptibilities to various poisons, diseases, and other problems. The ability of the surviving aphids to live was probably due to a gene or set of genes that the aphid has and can pass along to its offspring. If you apply the same chemical again, you'll again kill off the aphids that are susceptible to the poison, but now you'll have more aphids that are resistant to the chemical. The more applications you make of this pesticide, the fewer aphids you'll kill, until the pesticide is no better than water.

The genes that affect the resistance of an insect to one insecticide usually don't affect the ability of the insect to resist poisoning by another pesticide. Therefore, applying many different pesticides over time increases your chances of killing significant numbers of insects every time you spray. To take it just one step further, it's best to use different insecticide classes every time you spray. For example, if you were going to spray an insecticide on your marigolds three times a year, it would be best to use one spraying of an organophosphate, one spraying of a pyrethroid, and one spraying of a carbamate. (This is just an example; other insecticide classes could easily be used.)

BENEFITS Rotating pesticides avoids creating resistance and avoids the buildup of any one pesticide in the environment.

DRAWBACKS The biggest problem with chemical rotation is keeping track of the pesticides you've already applied. The best way to do this is by keeping a record sheet. A second problem is that when you use different chemicals, you'll sometimes be disappointed by the control that one of the chemicals offers and be tempted to go back to using one that works extremely well. Avoid this temptation. Repeated use of a single chemical practically guarantees that insects will develop resistance to this chemical and you'll end up with a mess on your hands in a few years.

THE BOTTOM LINE If you make only one or two (or better yet, zero!) insecticide applications a year, chemical rotation isn't particularly important for you. On the other hand, if you grow crops like roses that require constant insect control, you should be using chemical rotation techniques to avoid insecticide resistance.

THE BEST CHOICES FOR YOU

So who wins, organic or synthetic? This is entirely your decision, but for the record, I'm siding with the organic choices right up until you start looking at the pesticides. Once these things enter the picture, all bets are off for me. In my opinion, the best choice is not to apply insecticides at all if this is an option. As you've learned in this chapter, there are many ways to control insects that don't include any pesticides whatsoever. These should always be your first choice for insect control whenever possible. Sticky cards, traps, beneficial insects, choosing insect-resistant species: why wouldn't you try these options? The only reason I can think of is that the insect pests have overcome these methods. What then?

Is it really the end of the world if you lose a few of your vegetables or a few leaves from your azalea? If it is, your next step will probably be to go to the poisons section of the local hardware store or garden center. Here you'll find all kinds of options. Choose one by figuring out which pesticide will have the least potential impact on the environment while still taking care of your problem.

There are plenty of organic and synthetic insecticides out there that will provide instant (or at least pretty quick) gratification when they're sprayed, but, let's face it, these things were created to kill living organisms. As living organisms ourselves, we've got to wonder exactly how safe they are for us. While it may seem from this chapter that organic pesticides are generally safer, this is certainly not always the case, and in fact the scariest part of organic pesticides is that people tend to consider them safer simply because they're natural. Likewise, while synthetic pesticides might seem to be more effective than organics, this is not always the case. Organic pesticides such as Bt, pyrethrum, and rotenone compare favorably with most synthetic insecticides in terms of efficacy, but Bt is a relatively safe choice while rotenone is much, much worse.

If you decide to use a pesticide, I strongly suggest that you avoid becoming preoccupied with the organic versus synthetic debate and instead concentrate on how effective the insecticide will be and how safe it is. A final word on insecticides, which I've said before and will say again: be it organic or synthetic, never use any insecticide or other pesticide in a way contrary to what's written on that label.

6

Disease Control

A wide variety of disease control techniques are available, but the one that makes the most sense by far is simply keeping your plants healthy and vigorous. A healthy plant is less likely to develop disease than one that's malnourished and unhealthy. Plant health is best maintained through good soil, good watering techniques, and sufficient nutrition.

Keeping diseases away from healthy plants is an extremely important part of both conventional and organic gardening. Too often gardeners think they can save a diseased plant by pouring on the water and fertilizer (and sometimes pesticide). This is not the way to go. The best thing you can do with a diseased plant is to remove it from your garden to prevent the spread of disease to other plants. Additionally, be wary of adding vegetable material to your garden if it hasn't been well composted, as this material could introduce disease.

There aren't nearly as many methods for keeping plants disease free without chemicals as there are for keeping plants free of insects without chemicals. However, the methods we do have at our disposal are extremely effective, so don't be discouraged that there aren't more entries in the following section on organic cultural practices. In fact, the chapter in this book on soil enrichment and fertilization is as important to controlling diseases as this chapter, since those practices will help you keep your plants healthy, growing, and better able to shrug off diseases.

Once a disease starts to invade a garden, many people will consider applying chemicals to keep the problem at bay. Early detection of diseases is critical to being able to control them this way because applying sprays to plants that are already heavily infested with a disease is useless. The key to using chemical controls, be they organic or synthetic, is first to get rid of infested plants, leaves, and fruit and then to apply the chemical you've chosen to control the spread of the disease.

Organic and synthetic sprays have some distinct similarities and differences. One similarity that should be understood right off the bat is that both organic and synthetic sprays tend to be more effective at preventing diseases from taking hold in the first place than at curing them, so keeping a close eye on your plants is extremely important. That way you can respond before a potential disease situation spins hopelessly out of control.

Organic cultural practices

A number of simple cultural things can be done to reduce the chances that you'll be combating major disease problems. Most of them require some extra work, but some are pretty effort free. Organic sprays for controlling diseases are certainly available and some are quite effective, but the best organic methods are the techniques that don't include sprays.

Cleanliness

Rule number one in organic disease control is to remove diseased plants and plant materials such as diseased leaves (whether or not they've fallen from the plant) from the immediate area where healthy plants are growing. This alone will greatly diminish the need for other disease-control techniques. If a disease isn't around, it can't infect your plants—it's as simple as that. It's much more likely that a plant will become infected with a disease if it's attacked by a large number of bacteria or fungal spores than if it's attacked by a small number, so if you work to make sure that the potentially harmful fungi and bacteria in your garden are minimized, you're going to have much healthier plants. Besides keeping diseased plants out of your garden, keeping your gardening tools clean is also important. Pruners used to cut dead branches off of trees and shrubs can easily become contaminated with diseases that can spread from plant to plant. Sterilizing your pruners with bleach or some other sterilant as you go from tree to tree or shrub to shrub will help to reduce the spread of potentially damaging diseases such as fire blight, black spot, and rusts.

BENEFITS Keeping things clean will reduce the need for other disease controls and will also make your garden look nicer.

DRAWBACKS You actually have to go out and do some work; then again, if you don't like working and getting a little dirty, you probably don't like gardening anyway. Some people like to try to save diseased plants. If you're one of those people you might not like this disease control technique, but in almost all cases diseased plants aren't worth saving and end up causing more damage than they themselves are worth.

THE BOTTOM LINE Keeping diseased and potentially diseased plant materials out of your garden is a good way to prevent disease problems.

Compost tea and manure tea

Compost and manure teas are basically mixtures produced by placing either compost or manure (usually composted manure) in a bucket of water that includes some sugar and then allowing bacteria to grow. Sometimes air is bubbled through the system and sometimes it isn't. This tea is then applied to plants to help control disease. It seems that the bacteria (and perhaps the fungi) that grow in these systems are supposed to compete with bad bacteria and fungi, thereby keeping them from infesting your plants.

Some study results show that in some cases compost tea can help to control some diseases. A plethora of studies also demonstrate that compost tea is useless. I've frequently heard people who promote compost tea say that the reason this substance fails is that it's brewed incorrectly. This may well be true; however, if seasoned researchers can't figure out how to brew this stuff properly, I don't like the chances of the average Joe off the street successfully brewing this stuff.

Though I'm willing to say that compost tea may be able to help to control some diseases, particularly if it's made properly (Scheuerell and Mahaffee 2004), I'm not convinced that it can do so any more safely than other organic or synthetic sprays. Research shows that even though composting will kill off most pathogenic organisms such as *Escherichia coli* and salmonella, it's entirely possible that once that composted material hits the conditions in a compost tea brewer that are so beneficial for bacterial

growth, these disease-causing organisms will bounce back and reach potentially harmful levels (Duffy et al. 2004). This is potentially scary, scary
stuff, especially considering that certain organic gardeners and growers
use this brew to try to avoid the dangers of synthetic chemicals.

 The stuff might work. I'm especially optimistic about its potential for helping to control root rots. These teas will also
offer your plants a little shot of nutrition from the compost.

DRAWBACKS The potential for spreading nasty bacteria around and the inconsistent results that people have controlling different diseases make me very wary of these concoctions.

THE BOTTOM LINE Despite the potential of compost and manure teas, until research can show that a particular type of tea will work reliably
and doesn't contain human pathogens, I would strongly recommend stay-
ing away from these teas. Lots of articles, mostly nonscientific and unreliable, give all kinds of advice regarding which teas work best. Many of these
are in conflict with each other and don't provide sound reasons for their
recommendations. I find it difficult to cut through the rhetoric to get to
the science so instead choose to avoid this stuff altogether.

Polycultures and companion planting (intercropping)

The information presented in the insect control chapter on polycultures
applies here as well. Polycultures are present when more than one type of
plant is grown purposely in a particular area. This reduces the spread of
disease, because in many cases diseases are relatively host specific, meaning that they only infect some types of plants and not all. Indeed, most
home gardens are usually polycultures because they include so many diverse plants. Polycultures aren't perfect, but this method is certainly easy
to implement and even if it doesn't stop all of the disease in your garden, it
should slow the spread and severity of disease. Vegetable gardens are perhaps the most effective place to try a polyculture. Instead of planting tomatoes next to other tomatoes, intersperse them throughout your garden.
Then when a disease strikes, it will be more likely to affect a single tomato

plant rather than all of them, giving you a chance to remove the diseased tomato before the disease spreads. Roses are another plant likely to benefit from polycultures. Interspersing other plants among your roses will make it harder for fungal spores from diseases such as black spot and powdery mildew to get from one rose to another.

BENEFITS Polycultures are easy to implement and work quite well at limiting the spread of a disease should one occur. Polycultures also help to limit insect problems.

DRAWBACKS Harvest may be a little more difficult than if all plants of the same type were in one space. Likewise, planting many different types of plants together may not provide the uniform landscape that some gardeners are looking for.

THE BOTTOM LINE If it doesn't offend your aesthetic sensibilities, intercropping is a great way to limit disease spread.

Proper watering and fertilizing

I know that at first glance this one seems silly. Isn't it just common sense to water and fertilize properly? Yes, that's true, but why miss an opportunity to drive home an important point? Watering your plants properly will make it tougher for diseases to establish themselves on plant roots and cause you problems. Likewise, plants that are supplied with an appropriate amount of nutrition tend to be able to fight off, or even avoid, diseases more effectively than poorly fertilized plants. Remember, though, that proper watering and fertilizing doesn't mean overwatering and overfertilizing. Both could cause more problems than too little water and too little fertilizer.

So what exactly is the right amount of water and fertilizer? For water, make sure that the soil around your plants is moist but not wet. For fertilizer, use the lowest rate of fertilizer that's recommended on the fertilizer package unless you have a specific reason, such as a soil test, to apply more. If you're relying on compost as a means of providing nutrients to your plants, don't even worry about the fertilizer unless you know that you have a specific need for extra nutrition.

Applying the right amounts of water and fertilizer will not only help to control disease, it will also help to get your plants to grow their best.

 You have to pay attention to your plants to figure out when they need water and, potentially, fertilizer.

Pay attention to your plants' needs and good things will happen.

Planting disease-resistant cultivars

Perhaps the most common word in organic plant disease control is *resistance*. We all want plants that are resistant to whatever disease is most likely to affect them. For example, we want apples that are resistant to fire blight and scab, roses that are resistant to black spot and powdery mildew, and barberries that are resistant to rust. For most plants, when we refer to them as "disease resistant" we're only talking about a single disease, or perhaps two, rather than the whole spectrum of diseases that a plant might be exposed to. Additionally, resistance doesn't mean immunity. No matter how resistant an apple tree is to apple scab, if it's under enough stress because of overwatering, underfertilization, or any of a host of other problems, it can get apple scab.

Though resistance is an important part of any disease control program, organic or otherwise, it's actually a good thing that some people choose to plant varieties that aren't resistant to diseases; if we all planted the same resistant varieties of any plant, the disease the plant was resistant to would adapt to this resistance faster (it would have to for survival!) and the resistance would be rapidly overcome. It's only because we have an environment with both resistant and nonresistant plants that we're able to maintain resistant plants at all.

Some plants can be purchased with an indication right on the tag of what disease(s) the plant is resistant to. For example, when you purchase tomatoes, the symbol V on the tag indicates that the tomato will be resistant to verticillium wilt. Likewise, F indicates resistance to fusarium wilt, FF resistance to fusarium wilt race 1 and 2, N resistance to certain harmful nematodes, T resistance to tobacco mosaic virus, A resistance to alternaria (early blight), and TSW resistance to tomato spotted wilt virus. It's best to check with your local extension service to see which of these diseases is most prevalent in your area before you select a tomato based on these resistances.

BENEFITS Resistance is a disease control that's relatively cheap and easy to maintain—unless, of course, you decide to replant your entire garden with resistant varieties, which could become quite expensive. It certainly reduces the need for pesticides, and though resistance can fail, it doesn't do so frequently.

DRAWBACKS Disease resistance is usually to one or two diseases rather than all of the diseases that might affect a particular plant. Disease resistance is rarely perfect; in other words, if the conditions are right and the plant is under a great deal of stress, resistance is likely to break down.

THE BOTTOM LINE Disease-resistant plants are underutilized in gardens. They're an effective means to reduce losses due to bacteria and fungi, and though resistance is rarely perfect, it will usually mean significantly fewer headaches for the typical gardener.

Organic chemicals for disease control

A large number of pesticides are available to control diseases. In general these pesticides are safer for humans than insecticides simply because the organisms that these pesticides affect are so different from us, while insects are physiologically similar in many ways. Both synthetic and organic chemicals are ready and waiting to be used on disease, but if you've used the cultural controls listed earlier, you should significantly reduce and even eliminate your need for the chemicals described here. Please note that the following information in no way takes the place of a label. Labels need to be followed and are an integral part of using any pesticide, organic or synthetic, safely and effectively.

The organic arsenal includes a number of natural sprays that can be applied to plants to control diseases. Most of these sprays are used to prevent problems rather than cure them, so they're usually best applied when environmental conditions are conducive to the disease whether or not the disease has actually been observed on the plant, or at least before there's a major outbreak. Many synthetic disease control sprays are preventative as well, but some are also curative and so can be applied in response to a disease rather than prior to infection.

Many of the organic sprays used for disease control are quite effective and have been used for centuries; others are relatively new and some are not well tested. Though most of the organic controls are rather benign, some can be quite harmful to local environments if they're not used judiciously.

Some of the organic disease controls listed here aren't available to homeowners at the time of this writing; however, because these products may become available to the homeowner in the near future or even by the time this book is released, it seems best to include them.

Bacillus subtilis, Bacillus pumilus, and Trichoderma harzianum

The discovery and manipulation of *Bacillus thuringiensis* revolutionized insect control over the course of the twentieth century, and it seems possible and even likely that the manipulation of the bacterium *Bacillus subtilis* (EIQ 7.6) will do the same in the twenty-first. This bacterium was first registered for use in the United States in 1992 and currently at least four different products have been sold with this bacterium as the active ingredient, including Serenade and Rhapsody. When applied to seeds or roots this bacterium works by colonizing the root system of growing plants and inhibiting the growth of diseases. This inhibition seems to be due primarily to competition; in other words, this bacterium simply grows faster than the disease organisms that infect the plant can. A number of studies show that this bacterium is a potentially effective means of controlling many different root diseases. *Bacillus subtilis* can also be applied to foliage in certain situations and has been shown to be effective at controlling leaf spot and leaf blight in strawberries (Schilder, Gillett, and Sysak 2004) and somewhat effective on fire blight in apples, though not quite as effective as most conventional treatments (Aldwinckle and Penev 2004; Sundin and Ehret 2004). For powdery mildew, that ever-present disease feared by every gardener under the sun, it has been shown in various experiments to be anywhere from somewhat effective to ineffective and rarely rates up there with the best synthetic and organic sprays; nonetheless, it's an option that may provide some control depending on the circumstances. All in all, this product appears to have a promising future as a control for certain diseases in certain situations because of its efficacy against many different plant ailments and because it's currently considered to be quite safe.

Bacillus pumilus and *Trichoderma harzianum* are bacteria related to *Bacillus subtilis*. Though not as common as their relative, they have very similar attributes, being effective on a variety of diseases although not usually as effective as their synthetic counterparts. As with *Bacillus subtilis*, these disease controls are likely to be much more effective at controlling diseases that affect roots than diseases affecting leaves.

BENEFITS These bacteria should be reasonably safe and somewhat effective against many foliar diseases including fire blight. They appear to have much greater potential as a control for root diseases than for foliar diseases.

DRAWBACKS Though these products have proven themselves against some diseases, they're only rarely as effective as synthetic sprays or organic sprays, including copper or sulfur compounds. And although considered to be quite safe, these products haven't undergone safety testing as thorough as for synthetic chemicals.

THE BOTTOM LINE In a garden where you're trying to use the safest products available, these bacteria fit the bill, but disease control probably won't measure up to other organic and synthetic sprays, especially if you're looking at leaf rather than soil disease.

Bordeaux mix

I really enjoy old remedies with good stories and Bordeaux mix has one of the best. One of my great joys in life is to take up an hour of my students' time every year reviewing the discovery of this fungicide.

It all started with the need to control an infestation of pests that were known for reducing grape yield in the Bordeaux region of France. These pests consumed great quantities of food, carried themselves on two feet, and were known as people. Over the years a variety of techniques had been attempted to control people nicking grapes from vines, the most common being a spray of verdigris (the green coating that accumulates on copper that's exposed to the weather), which was applied to grapevines planted along roadsides. Verdigris was, however, somewhat expensive, so over time a cheaper replacement was developed that was made of a mixture of lime, water, and copper sulfate. This mixture was particularly nasty looking, with a milky blue-green hue, though it was relatively safe for the plant under most conditions and easy to wash off. As a spray on plants it proved to have the desired effect and reduced the amount of feeding by humans. (Would you want to eat grapes covered with a milky blue-green coating?)

But how did this mixture come to be known as a fungicide? It happened when downy mildew started to infest the grape-growing regions of Europe. You see, downy mildew isn't a native pest of grapes in Europe, but is, rather, a pest native to America. The Bordeaux region in France was one of the first areas in Europe to be infested with this disease, which appeared around 1878, perhaps because of experiments with American grape varieties by grape growers in that region. In 1882 the conditions for the spread of downy mildew were extremely favorable and a great number of grapes were lost; however, the grapevines along the roads of Bordeaux were relatively mildew free and retained most of their foliage and grapes. It seemed that these grapes survived when so many others did not because of the mixture of lime and copper sulfate that had been sprayed on them. Alexis Millardet, a well-known researcher at the time, was one of the first to notice the effects of this mixture and is given credit today for discovering Bordeaux mix, a fantastic fungicide that's really nothing more than a mixture of water, lime, and copper sulfate.

Bordeaux mix, though a simple mixture, does have some properties that need to be addressed before you run willy-nilly to the store to buy it, as should be evident by its EIQ of 47.8. Copper sulfate can be quite toxic to humans and isn't something you should be spraying every day. This mixture lasts for only a short time on plants and washes off relatively easily. Bordeaux mix affects bacteria as well as fungi and so can be used against such diseases as fire blight. It's classified as a protectant, meaning that it will only protect the area of the plant that it comes into contact with and won't cure an infection that's already present. Bordeaux mix is comparable to synthetic protectants (covered below) in terms of its efficacy against diseases in most tests, but it may need to be applied more frequently than these synthetic disease controls and may cause leaf damage to plants if it's applied when temperatures are in the mid 80s or higher or below about 50 degrees F when humidity is high.

BENEFITS That this fungicide is still used after more than a century should tell you something about its efficacy. Bordeaux mix is an effective and relatively inexpensive disease control. Many other organic fungicides are only effective on fungi, as the name "fungicide" implies; Bordeaux mix is effective against bacteria as well as fungi, so can be used to help control such bacterial diseases as fire blight.

DRAWBACKS The toxicity of copper sulfate to most mammals and aquatic creatures makes this fungicide somewhat more dangerous to apply than many others. This mixture also has the potential to burn plants, especially under high temperature conditions or when temperatures are low (below 50 degrees F) and humidity is high. It's also possible that if the mixture is used too frequently, copper will build up in the soil and could potentially damage plants, as indicated in the upcoming section on copper.

THE BOTTOM LINE Applied properly and with the precautions that should be taken with applications of any pesticide, Bordeaux mix is a useful tool in controlling disease. However, its toxicity and potential for injuring plants need to be taken into account when deciding whether this is the appropriate fungicide for the situation.

Copper

Copper, glimpsed previously as a constituent of Bordeaux mix, is also a key component of other disease controls. Fungicides including the compounds copper hydroxide (EIQ 33.3) and copper sulfate (EIQ 47.8) are commonly used by organic growers faced with a wide variety of fungal diseases. These sprays, like those containing sulfur, listed below, need to be applied before a disease attacks because they affect the germination of fungal spores. Copper compounds tend to be as effective as synthetic fungicides, though they're often more dangerous depending on the synthetic that they're compared to.

Copper sulfate in particular is known to be quite toxic to humans and other mammals and is especially toxic to fish and other aquatic organisms, so any application of this fungicide around water should be undertaken with care. In the environment this fungicide has problems that need to be taken into account before it's applied. In fact, studies show that repeated use of copper compounds may result in increased concentrations of this element in the soil, which can affect beneficial soil microorganisms and even retard the growth of copper-sensitive crops (Epstein and Bassein 2001). In practice most gardeners won't apply enough copper to cause this to occur; nonetheless, it's always prudent to apply any poison, and especially one with as much potential for damage as this, with great care and restraint.

BENEFITS Copper compounds are very effective at controlling plant diseases and are usually considered to be as effective as synthetic disease controls.

DRAWBACKS The worst problem with copper is its potential for damaging aquatic environments if it's misapplied. Copper may need to be applied repeatedly to maintain disease control and has the potential to harm the garden if applied again and again over the years, but this shouldn't affect the gardener who applies copper judiciously. Copper compounds are very dangerous if they're ingested.

THE BOTTOM LINE Copper compounds can be quite dangerous to both the environment and human health if misapplied, but they tend to be very effective at controlling diseases. I shy away from copper compounds, including Bordeaux mix, simply because of their potential health effects and environmental concerns.

Lime sulfur

Lime sulfur isn't a chemical that you commonly find on the garden center shelves anymore, but a good Internet search will reveal places to purchase this product. Two people claim to have used lime sulfur first: Grison, the head gardener at Versailles, France, in 1851, and one Lawrence Young of Louisville, Kentucky, in 1845 (Lodeman 1906). Used heavily in the late 1800s and early 1900s as both a fungicide and an insecticide that was particularly effective on scale insects, this chemical has probably seen the height of its use, for reasons that will soon become clear.

Lime sulfur is a mixture of hydrated lime and sulfur and is effective on a wider variety of diseases than sulfur used alone. Lime sulfur has the same temperature drawback that sulfur and copper do in that it shouldn't be applied if temperatures are above about 80 degrees F. Some research investigating how well lime sulfur compares to sulfur in preventing apple scab has shown that lime sulfur is more effective but is also more likely to hurt the tree and may even lead to season-long effects such as reduced leaf size (Holb, De Jong, and Heijne 2003). This product's degree of phytotoxicity (how poisonous it is to plants) makes it less than attractive to most gardeners.

BENEFITS Lime sulfur will work against many diseases, often as effectively as synthetic fungicides.

DRAWBACKS This chemical is more likely than many of the other organic and synthetic chemical fungicides to damage plants, especially under very warm or hot conditions.

THE BOTTOM LINE Even though sulfur won't be as effective as this product, it's a better choice in most situations because of the potential for damage that lime sulfur presents.

Oxytetracycline

Oxytetracycline, an antibiotic that's usually sold as Mycoshield, isn't commonly available to gardeners; rather, it's a product employed by commercial growers that may one day be available to consumers for home use. This antibacterial compound was discovered in the 1950s and comes from a fungus called *Streptomyces rimosus*. It's very effective against many bacterial problems such as bacterial spot and fire blight. Oxytetracycline is currently available for commercial organic production in the United States but isn't considered acceptable as an organic disease control in Europe.

This is an effective way to control bacterial problems, the most common of which is fire blight.

This is an antibiotic. Spraying antibiotics will affect beneficial bacteria as well as harmful ones. This product is useful against fire blight and a few other bacterial problems but really isn't intended for fungal diseases such as powdery mildew, black spot, or rust.

This product works for organic producers who need to control fire blight. If and when it becomes labeled for gardeners, it may be a good way to control bacterial diseases in the yard, but I worry about spraying antibiotics because of the buildup of resistance that this type of use could lead to over time.

Potassium bicarbonate and sodium bicarbonate

Baking soda (sodium bicarbonate) and its close relative potassium bicarbonate have been known to be effective against powdery mildew since the 1920s. These organic fungicides are sold under a variety of trade names, including Milstop, Kaligreen, and Armicarb. Homemade disease control mixtures can be made with a tablespoon of baking soda, a tablespoon of some type of oil such as vegetable oil, and a few drops of dishwashing soap. Do be aware that this homemade spray may burn plants and probably won't be as effective as commercial sprays.

Although studies generally show that these fungicides work against powdery mildew, they tend to be less effective than synthetics such as chlorothalonil. The most effective formulations of these chemicals include oils and soaps that enable the sodium or potassium bicarbonate to be applied more evenly across the leaf surface. Both of these bicarbonates can cause damage to plants if they're overapplied. Though these chemicals are often applied to roses to control black spot, they're generally not considered very effective at stopping this disease and have been known since the mid-1920s to have only marginal activity against it (Massey 1925). These products are considered relatively safe for the environment; potassium bicarbonate has an EIQ of 8.

 These are relatively safe fungicides that are reasonably effective on a wide variety of diseases.

DRAWBACKS Many people may not be satisfied with the level of disease control that these products offer, especially considering that they're known to not be particularly effective against black spot on roses.

THE BOTTOM LINE For most gardeners these products will provide satisfactory but not great control of most diseases. This, combined with the fact that these products are relatively safe, makes them a good choice for most gardeners.

Sulfur

The oldest pesticide still in common use in Western culture is sulfur. Sulfur has been known as a pesticide since Greek and Roman times, when it was used to control rust on wheat as well as other diseases and insects (a fact referred to in the ancient writings of Cato and Varro and of Pliny). Besides rust, sulfur also controls diseases such as black spot and powdery mildew. This element works to control fungi by stopping the germination of fungal spores, so it must be on the plant before the disease that it's supposed to protect against. Besides working well as a fungicide, sulfur will also have some effects on certain pest arthropods such as spider mites, psyllids, and thrips, as well as some beneficial insects. Sulfur (EIQ 45.5) is a relatively safe compound that nevertheless has a few major problems, one of these being its propensity to burn plants at temperatures exceeding about 80 degrees F and for reacting poorly with oil sprays. Another problem is that sulfur may be toxic to beneficial insects. Sulfur is considered a good fungicide that works as well as most synthetic chemicals, but it must be applied many times over the course of a season because of its propensity to wash off of plants. Besides its fungicidal effects, sulfur is also used for reducing the pH of soils; it has been established that over the course of a few years some soils will become more acidic in locations where sulfur is used regularly as a fungicide (Majule, Topper, and Nortcliff 1997).

 BENEFITS Sulfur is a relatively safe fungicide that's as effective as most synthetic fungicides. Some insect pests will also be affected.

 DRAWBACKS Sulfur must be reapplied frequently and under suitable environmental conditions or else it may fail to control disease or damage plants. Repeated heavy use can lead to soil acidification in some situations.

 Sulfur is a good replacement for synthetic fungicides if it's used wisely.

Synthetic chemicals for disease control

Synthetic fungicides have been around for a long time, though certainly not as long as many of the organic ones. One of the first of the synthetic fungicides was thiram, introduced in the early 1930s and still available today as the active ingredient in some of the fungicides you can purchase in garden centers.

Synthetic fungicides can be split into three major groups: (1) plant activators, which stimulate plants to defend themselves, (2) protectants, which prevent disease from infesting plants by blocking its entry into the surface of the leaf or roots, and (3) systemics, which actually enter the plant's vascular system to defend it from disease. All of these different groups have their benefits and drawbacks, as we'll see in the upcoming sections.

Plant activators

What if there were something you could spray on your plants that would make them think that a disease was coming? It might stimulate the plant to get ready for the disease, kind of like a vaccine. A few products like this, reported to increase the ability of plants to fight off diseases, are available on the market. Many of these products are considered organic, but a few are also synthetic. Plant activators may include a number of active ingredients, including beta-1,3 glucan, harpin, and acibenzolar-S-methyl, sold as Vacciplant, Messenger, and Actigard, respectively. These compounds are supposed to prepare plants for impending disease by promoting systemic acquired resistance (SAR)—which, in a nutshell, means that they work by stimulating the plant to produce defensive compounds that in turn protect the plant from disease.

I have tried both harpin and acibenzolar-S-methyl in tests against black spot and powdery mildew on roses and have found that harpin was generally not very effective at controlling either disease, while acibenzolar-S-methyl, though not as good as most synthetics, showed some promise. In general, the results generated by other researchers have followed the same lines. Acibenzolar-S-methyl seems to have real potential for disease control and appears to be particularly effective at controlling bacterial diseases such as fire blight. The other compounds simply haven't reliably demonstrated over the course of many studies that they can help plants to avoid disease. Based on the available data, plant activators appear to be relatively safe products.

An interesting point here is that acibenzolar-S-methyl is a chemical analogue of aspirin, which basically just means that it's pretty similar to it. So does that mean that aspirin can be effective at controlling disease? Actually, some research out there points to just that. Back in the 1970s some research conducted by R. F. White (1979) showed that injecting aspirin into tobacco would help it to resist tobacco mosaic virus. Since then a number of other studies have shown that applications of aspirin may help to protect plants against various diseases (Malamy and Kessig 1992), though all cases where aspirin is tried as a disease control certainly don't have fantastic results.

 These products are considered relatively safe and at least one of them, acibenzolar-S-methyl, seems to be reasonably effective.

 The efficacy of these products is probably not as good as that of more typical organic or synthetic sprays.

BOTTOM LINE I like acibenzolar-S-methyl. No, it's not organic, but it's a relatively safe compound that helps defend plants against disease. We need more research into compounds that are safe and effective, with the emphasis on safe. I think it's fun to experiment with aspirin, but I'm not sold on its ability to control disease quite yet.

Protectants

By far the most common types of synthetic disease controls available today are protectants. Protectants were the first synthetic fungicides to become available and include such compounds as mancozeb (EIQ 14.6), thiram

(EIQ 32.5), and ferbam (EIQ 28.8). Among the protectants you're most likely to see on a garden center shelf, chlorotholonil (EIQ 40.1) and captan (EIQ 15.8) lead the list, but others are available. One of the biggest advantages of protectants is that they don't tend to promote disease resistance, something that many of the systemic fungicides do. Perhaps the most important reason for the lack of resistance to protectants is that with protectants you get many escapes. Let me explain. When a protectant fungicide is used, only those surfaces covered with the fungicide are protected from disease, and any area that's missed (as some are sure to be, with a spray) will provide a small safe haven for disease. This safe haven means that the disease can survive without having to develop a resistance to the pesticide, and the survival of nonresistant disease organisms insures that the protectant will continue to be effective in the future. Systemic disease controls, on the other hand, don't allow escapes. The entire plant is treated with the chemical, so the disease attempting to circumvent the effects of the chemical needs to develop resistance to it in order to survive. Hence, while protectants allow a little more disease on the plants they're applied to, they also run less risk of resistance problems in the future.

BENEFITS Few diseases have developed a great deal of resistance to these products. Synthetic protectants tend to be quite effective at controlling disease if used properly and can generally be expected to work as well as or better than most of the organic fungicides, with less chance of damaging your crops. Also, less of these products than of organic fungicides usually needs to be applied.

DRAWBACKS Protectants have a wide range of degrees of safety for both humans and the environment. Some are considered relatively safe and some aren't. Because they don't get into the plant's vascular system, they don't provide complete control of diseases.

 I like protectant fungicides and usually use them instead of systemics simply because of the resistance issue.

Systemics

Synthetic systemic fungicides first appeared in the 1960s. They were extremely popular because they would protect every portion of the plant and were amazingly effective. Unfortunately, what we usually eventually find out after a few years of using amazingly effective pesticides is that pests become amazingly resistant to these chemicals, and this case was no different. These fungicides, if used repeatedly, have significant problems with pests becoming resistant to them. In some cases the use of these fungicides will allow other diseases that you may not have even noticed before to suddenly become resistant. For example, you could treat a rose repeatedly for black spot and suddenly see an onset of anthracnose. In this case you would have successfully controlled the disease you wanted to control, but your repeated use of a fungicide would have allowed another disease to develop resistance and become a problem.

Systemic fungicides work by moving through a plant's vascular system to almost every portion of the plant to protect it from disease. This may or may not include the fruit we eat from various plants. Where it does include fruit, the chemical is usually all but gone by the time the fruit is harvested as long as proper application methods have been followed (in other words: read the label).

Systemic fungicides will also affect mycorrhizae, those fungi that live in the ground and normally infect your plant, helping it to take up nutrition from the soil. Some studies have shown that these fungicides can actually stimulate mycorrhizal infection (Groth and Martinson 1983), which is a good thing. But more commonly these fungicides inhibit mycorrhizal infection (Dodd and Jeffries 1989; Jabaji-Hare and Kendrick 1987). This makes systemic fungicides even less palatable.

Some systemic fungicides have curative properties—in other words, they can actually help to cure a plant of a disease it has already contracted. These curative properties are usually overestimated by gardeners, who think that black spot will just disappear if they apply these chemicals, but that really isn't the case at all. In most situations the best a curative can do is to stop mild infections from spreading too much.

Systemic fungicides are likely to provide protection from diseases for a longer period of time than protectants because they're actually present inside the plant rather than just on the surface of a leaf. This means that they're protected somewhat from environmental conditions that might wash them away or degrade them (sunlight breaks down many chemicals).

If you decide to go with systemic fungicides, you should use pesticide rotation because of the problems with resistance that many systemic fungicides have. Be sure to apply different fungicides over the course of a year rather than always applying the same one, even if you know that one of your fungicides works better than another. The use of a single fungicide will promote resistance among the diseases that you're trying to control. Instead, pick out two or three systemics and apply a different one when you feel the need to treat for a disease. In the long run this will keep all of your fungicides effective.

Some of the more common systemic fungicides include aluminum tris, benomyl (EIQ 52.6), myclobutanil (EIQ 33), tebuconazole (EIQ 40.3), thiophanate methyl (EIQ 22.42), triadimefon (EIQ 30.7), and triforine (EIQ 41.2). Some diseases have resistance to the activity of each of these, so these systemics might fail in any given situation. That said, they're also likely to give better control than a protectant if resistance isn't present. Unfortunately, the only way to know whether resistance is present is to use the fungicide and wait to see whether the disease infects the plant.

BENEFITS Systemic disease controls keep plants very clean when resistance isn't present and can be extremely effective.

DRAWBACKS Diseases regularly controlled with systemics tend to develop resistance to these chemicals relatively quickly. Additionally, these disease controls may adversely affect the beneficial fungi, mycorrhizae, that would normally infect your plants.

THE BOTTOM LINE If you want to keep your plants pristine, without a single blemish, these products are the best way to go as long as the disease you're trying to control isn't resistant to the systemic fungicide you're using. This resistance is the reason I usually avoid these fungicides.

THE BEST CHOICES FOR YOU

The best choice is almost always to minimize your use of fungicides whenever possible. This is best done by selecting disease-resistant plants for your garden, by growing healthy plants and ensuring that they have sufficient water and fertilizer to stand up to low levels of disease, and by keeping your garden free of diseased plants and fresh vegetable waste (which may contain disease and so infect other plants).

Before you even think about using a fungicide, you need to identify the problem that you're trying to either control or prevent. This book is about controls and not disease identification, so I'm not going to spend time covering the diseases that might be attacking your fruits, vegetables, or ornamentals. What I will do is to point you to your local agricultural extension service, which should be able to provide you with some resources and insight on identifying the pests you might have. After your extension service helps you figure out what you've got, or at least helps you figure out a good resource to help you figure out what you've got, then they may recommend some controls to vanquish the problem, and that's where this book comes in, helping you to decide which controls make the most sense for you. If you've established that you want to control a disease with a pesticide, the next step is to work out which one makes the most sense for you based on the safety of the chemical, how well it controls the disease, and what its environmental effects are.

Where health and safety are major concerns and you're dealing with diseases that are attacking the plant's leaves, the organic fungicide sulfur is a good choice along with the synthetic fungicide chlorothalonil. Both of these fungicides are quite effective against fungal disease and are considered to be relatively safe to humans if used according to the label. Do be aware that chlorothalonil is a true fungicide—in other words, it's not going to affect bacterial diseases such as fire blight. Checking the label to see which diseases are supposed to be controlled by any given chemical is imperative in any situation to avoid potential problems. Also, though I've pointed out sulfur and chlorothalonil for the sake of listing two compounds that are very useful, in many instances there might be better chemicals, depending on your particular situation. Get to know the folks at your local extension service; it's only going to help your ability to deal with problems.

Here's something you need to think about before treating anything for a disease. If you see blemishes or spots that indicate a disease, you won't be able to make these spots that have already appeared go away. Once these blemishes have formed, you can't do a thing about them except perhaps to stop their spread. Hence, timing is your biggest issue. The most effective time to treat with a disease control chemical is when the infection is hitting or before. So if you want to keep your plants pristine, your best bet is to know which diseases are likely to strike when and then to treat with a prophylactic application of a fungicide. This could actually mean lots and lots of spraying, and it's a method I don't like for that very reason, but it's a method frequently used by organic growers who need to get control of diseases before they go too far. The better option, in my opinion, is simply to decide to accept a certain amount of damage and not make any fungicide applications unless damage is about to cross that threshold.

If you're dealing with root diseases, some of the more interesting and potentially helpful disease control choices include bacterial controls such as *Bacillus subtilis*, which is difficult for the home gardener to find. Synthetic fungicides that protect roots aren't readily available to homeowners, though commercial growers do have some options. If you know that a plant has a root rot problem, the best thing to do is to remove the plant, alter the conditions of the soil (usually root rots are encouraged by soil that's too wet or too dry) or select a plant that can better tolerate the planting conditions, and try again. Another option for root problems is to try solarization, which was mentioned earlier in the chapter on weed control.

If your primary concern is keeping your plants spotless, the systemic fungicides are probably right for you. I'm not really a proponent of systemics in general, but if you want to keep a plant blemish free they're the way to go. If you want to keep a plant pristine by using organic or protectant fungicides, understand that there's the distinct possibility that you'll damage your plants simply because of the number of sprays you'll have to apply.

If you definitely want to go organic, sulfur and copper work very well to limit the spread of diseases if they're applied regularly and soon after signs of infection occur. Copper fungicides, including Bordeaux mix, have the distinct drawback of being quite toxic if misapplied, so use them with care. Both sulfur and copper can have lasting effects in the garden if they're overused because they may build up in the soil, so if you want to use one of these organic controls be sure to pay attention to the label and to apply them as infrequently as you can. Both of these chemicals are most dangerous when applied at heavy concentrations year after year in production settings, something that doesn't usually happen in the typical garden. As long as you're using these compounds judiciously, you should be OK.

7

Controlling Birds, Deer, Rodents, and Mollusks

Though insects and diseases are certainly important problems around the garden, a host of other pests can also infiltrate, irritate, and just plain frustrate any gardener. Some of the greatest pests in the garden are of the two-winged or four-legged rather than the six- or eight-legged variety. These pests can be very difficult to control for a variety of reasons, not the least of which is that many of the poisons we'd like to use on them are, unsurprisingly, very toxic to us as well. Because of this toxicity, and also because we feel a curious empathy toward mammals and birds that we don't seem to feel toward things like insects, slugs, spiders, and fungi, we've developed a variety of repellents that deter rather than kill these creatures. Most of these deterrents are organic rather than synthetic, and most of them are not only safe but also quite effective. The synthetics, on the other hand, tend to be rather toxic as well as effective and certainly provide the satisfaction of knowing that you've killed the pest.

Bird control: The organic choices

Don't you hate it when you've got a huge crop of something all ready to be picked and then a bunch of birds, usually crows or sparrows, decides that your crop looks pretty tasty, too? Fortunately, many organic controls and a few synthetic ones are available to deter these pests. None of the organic controls will keep the birds away for a particularly long time, but they can be effective in the short term. The few synthetic controls are by and large not available to homeowners, with good reason.

The organic choices for bird control provide the safest and most reasonable option to keep these pests away from your crops in most situations.

None of them is foolproof, but used wisely they can provide at least a modicum of control.

Netting

Bird netting covers the trees or plants that you want to protect from the villainous beaks of birds. These nets are coarse enough to let sunlight in but tight enough to keep most birds out. When tested, nets are quite effective, though some losses can still be expected because birds can reach in through the small holes in the fabric to take at least a few pecks. When blueberry losses to birds were examined over a three-year period in Quebec, between 6 and 9 percent of the crop was lost with bird netting while between 24 and 64 percent of the crop was lost without bird netting. In fact, when bird netting was compared to the synthetic bird repellent methiocarb and untreated plants, the bird netting was much more effective than the synthetic bird repellent; the repellent resulted in losses that weren't significantly different from those sustained by the untreated plants (Vincent and Lareau 1993), so the answer here is pretty clear. Using bird netting is going to help to control those birds.

BENEFITS This stuff works and will last for much longer than most other controls.

DRAWBACKS Some loss will occur because these nets obviously need holes to allow sun and water through and to allow insects into the structure to pollinate if the net is placed on the plant early in the season (which isn't usually necessary, as birds tend to eat fruits rather than flowers). These nets are somewhat less than attractive.

THE BOTTOM LINE These nets can be kind of ugly and they won't provide perfect control, but then neither do repellents. If you can put up with their unsightliness, these nets are a good idea.

Roost inhibitors

Polybutene and polyisobutylene are sticky substances that while synthetically produced are used by organic gardeners because they can be used in such small quantities and in specific areas. The sticky texture of these products is supposed to irritate the bird's feet and encourage it to find somewhere else to roost. I haven't seen extensive testing of these products, but they're used by various airports to reduce their bird problems.

Other roost inhibitors that you can purchase include stiff strands of wire that make it uncomfortable for birds to perch and a sort of electric fence system that shocks birds when they try to roost. Though these methods seem rather aggressive, they're both reported to work.

 Roost inhibitors are relatively safe products that work by making a place uncomfortable for birds to land or perch.

 Polybutene and polyisobutylene are synthetic products, in the strictest sense of the word, which may bother some hardcore organic advocates. Additionally, these products can be difficult to wash off, and the wire and electric devices can cause injuries, especially to young children, so they need to be placed with care.

The sticky products haven't been tested enough to get a firm grasp of exactly how effective they are or how long they last. I've seen the wire products function effectively in a city environment and would expect them to function well in confined spaces where the birds would be forced to contact the wires. Similarly, electric fencing specifically created for birds should be very effective in spaces that are small enough to force contact.

Sonic bird repellents

Sonic repellents emit sounds that are within our hearing range and that of most pest birds. Unfortunately, these sounds are usually irritating to humans as well as birds. Birds do become accustomed over time to noises that machines generate (Blokpoel 1976; Woronecki 1988), so the ability of these machines to keep birds out of an area is limited to a few days or weeks.

These repellents do work for a short period of time and have few side effects as long as people aren't forced to listen to them all day.

DRAWBACKS One of the few side effects you may face is an irritated neighbor. Birds become habituated to sounds rapidly so control is usually limited to a few days or weeks.

THE BOTTOM LINE If you need to keep birds out of an area for a short period of time (right before harvesting apples, for example) and don't have any neighbors who will be annoyed by the sounds, sonic repellents may be the right choice for you.

Taste aversions

There are feeding deterrents for birds just as there are for deer and rodents. The most common of these is methyl anthranilate, which is available commercially in a number of different formulations. This chemical is derived from grapes, so it's considered relatively safe. While aerosols that incorporate methyl anthranilate into a fog have been shown to be effective at inhibiting birds (Stevens and Clark 1998), this compound has rarely proven effective at deterring birds from feeding when it's applied directly to plants—which is, unfortunately, the way most people would prefer to apply it. It has proven ineffective at protecting rice and sunflower fields (Werner et al. 2005) as well as cherries, blueberries, and grapes (Curtis et al. 1994). Still, RejeX-it Crop Guardian, a product that incorporates this chemical into microscopic spheres in a process called microencapsulation, may have some potential since a microencapsulated form of methyl anthranilate did significantly reduce bird damage in at least one experiment (Curtis et al. 1994).

BENEFITS If you purchase methyl anthranilate as a fogging agent to repel groups of birds, you should have some success. Additionally, some studies have shown some short-term successes from applying this product directly to plants.

 DRAWBACKS This chemical hasn't proven to be consistently effective at controlling bird feeding.

 THE BOTTOM LINE Methyl anthranilate won't be consistently effective at repelling birds if you apply it directly to plants. However, if you buy it as a fogging agent you may be able to deter birds from coming near a particular piece of land. This product is considered to be relatively safe.

Ultrasonic bird repellents

Among the most common repellents you can buy for birds are devices that emit very high frequency sounds. After reading about sonic repellents you may wonder how effective it is to irritate a bird's eardrums. If sonic repellents work for only a short span of time, why should we expect ultrasonic repellents to be any different? Though I've seen all kinds of testimonials on these devices, I find it hard to believe that they actually work, because the natural range of hearing for pest birds is about the same as our range of hearing (Brand and Kellogg 1939). Researchers testing these devices almost invariably find them to be all but useless (Griffiths 1988; Woronecki 1988), so all they really do is make you feel like you've done something to control the problem, a feeling that quickly departs after the birds come back.

 These little contraptions can look pretty neat.

 Many studies have been done but no research evidence that I'm aware of demonstrates that these products actually work.

 Don't waste your time.

Visual scare devices

Scarecrows are the oldest form of visual scare device and have evolved from simple straw dolls on sticks to ribbons of flashing lights and spinning disco balls. But have you ever noticed that pictures of scarecrows often show a crow sitting on the figure's shoulder? Visual scare devices, like sonic repellents, tend to work for a short time and then fail as the birds get used to them. A study in New Zealand found that sparrows, blackbirds, and starlings become accustomed to eye-spotted beach ball scare devices within four weeks and then start to feed on the grapes that the device is supposed to be protecting (McLennan, Langham, and Porter 1995), and other studies using caged doves found similar results (Nakamura et al. 1995). In a test comparing sonic, ultrasonic, and visual scare devices, the sonic devices worked for the longest time, followed by the visual scare devices (Woronecki 1988).

 Visual devices aren't likely to bother anybody too much and appear to be effective for at least a short period of time.

 Visual devices may work for as long as a month but shouldn't be expected to work longer.

These devices make a lot of sense if you need to keep the birds away for just a week or three. Any longer than that and you may be in trouble.

Bird control: The synthetic choices

Many of the synthetic choices for bird control that you're likely to see are available only to licensed pesticide applicators for specific purposes. These choices usually consist of chemicals that are normally used for other purposes such as fungicides and insecticides and that have coincidentally been found to be either poisonous or repellent to birds as well. Synthetic controls can be quite effective but also can have effects beyond what's acceptable to most people. If a major infestation of birds is causing you problems and organic controls aren't working, the best course for you to follow is to contact a local pest control company and have them assess the problem. Do be aware that some of the pest controls used by professional companies may include poisons, so be sure to find out exactly what products they're using and where they're planning to use them.

Deer control

The most common pest question I get is how to control deer. The best way, without a doubt, is to install a very tall fence (ten or so feet tall) that slopes outward, toward the direction from which the deer will be trying to enter—and you know what? Some deer will still jump that fence. Chain-link fences are usually considered best because they offer the least opportunity for deer to slip through gaps. Wooden fences will work but have been known to have sections kicked out by deer that want to get through. Plastic fences usually aren't effective at stopping deer because over time they crack and split. Electric fences can work, but oftentimes deer will simply learn that they just need to jump a little higher to get over the fence.

Besides fences, there aren't a whole lot of surefire cures. There are few synthetic methods of getting rid of deer, with the exception of some poisons that aren't available to the typical gardener, and some noxious chemicals that may be present in some repellents. Hunting is certainly a method of reducing deer problems, but be sure to check into state and local laws and ordinances that may restrict the usefulness of this method.

A wide variety of things can be used to keep deer out of the garden, from concoctions that are supposed to bother their senses of smell and taste to deterrents that are supposed to actually scare the deer away. Any of these concoctions might work for you, but they might also fail. The efficacy of deer control efforts can vary seasonally; if you're trying to control deer in the spring and summer it's generally easier than if you're trying to control them in the winter. This is because in the spring and summer, deer should be able to find something else to munch on besides those plants they're repelled from; in the winter deer can't find as much food, so they're willing to put up with plants that taste worse in order to avoid starvation.

Baited electric wires

Most people who have used electric wire to keep deer away know that this will work once and then the deer will jump right over that wire and eat whatever they want from the garden, but there's a way to set up an electric wire to repel deer that's much more effective. In fact, I used it back when I was a graduate student to protect cowpeas from deer and was extremely impressed with it. One of the first to report this method was C. L. Kinsey (1976), who used this practice to control white-tailed deer. Many researchers have found this practice to be quite effective since then (Hygnstrom and Craven 1988; Porter 1983), but this shouldn't be considered a surefire cure.

A baited electric fence is set up by stringing an electric wire around the area you want to protect. The wire should be set at about the height of a deer's nose, three or four feet high. Dab a little bit of peanut butter on it every few feet, hang some plastic flagging tape from the wire so that you're sure the deer will see it, and then turn the wire on. The deer will smell the peanut butter, go over to the electric wire, and take a taste. They'll get shocked right on the nose, sending them running. Deer can become accustomed to this technique over time, but more often than not it's successful.

 This technique has been as successful as any for keeping deer out of small plots of land.

 You need an outlet or a solar-powered electric fence for this to work. This technique tends to be most effective on small plots rather than large areas. Electric fences are dangerous to children, people with heart conditions, and potentially others.

 This technique is great if you have a small area to protect, don't have many close neighbors, and do have a source of power for the fence.

Commercial repellents

Deer repellents from the store like Hinder, Deer Away, and many others often do a fine job of keeping deer away from your plants, especially in the spring when other food choices are available to them. These products have most of the same things in them that homemade sprays do, like eggs (often called putrescent egg solids) and hot sauce; some deer repellents use synthetic chemicals such as ammonia, which has a strong odor. Despite the fact that you pay good money for such repellents, they're not guaranteed to work. Their big advantage over homemade sprays is that they tend to last longer because they contain substances that help them to stick more efficiently to the surface you're trying to protect. If you decide to go the commercial route you're usually best off selecting a spray that includes putrescent egg solids, which have proven to be one of the best deer repellents (Lemieux, Maynard, and Johnson 2000).

 Commercial repellents can work and tend to last longer than homemade repellents.

DRAWBACKS These repellents tend to smell bad, though I've never seen them actually drive people out of an area. These sprays can be expensive when compared with homemade sprays. Though these sprays may last longer than homemade sprays, they'll rarely last the whole winter for most locations.

THE BOTTOM LINE These are generally good products that will reduce deer feeding in most situations, but be aware that no repellent is perfect and that over time and as deer become more desperate for food, these repellents are more likely to fail.

Homemade repellents

Deer repellents composed of things from the fridge may work to repel deer for a short period of time until they wash off the plants. These repellents often include eggs and/or hot peppers pureed in water and applied to plants to bother the deer's sense of smell and taste. Usually anywhere from four to sixteen eggs and a few tablespoons of hot sauce or pureed garlic are mixed with a gallon of water and spritzed on the plants from a handheld sprayer. Generally these concoctions won't last for longer than a week or two after they're applied, but some people claim that adding an anti-transpirant such as Wilt Pruf to the mixture will make it last longer (while at the same time making it more injurious to plants). Eggs are known to be good animal repellents, so it's likely that these repellents will work in the spring months when deer can choose something else to eat, but these sprays are unlikely to last for an entire winter.

BENEFITS Homemade sprays to control deer do tend to be cheaper than commercial ones and do tend to repel deer to some degree.

DRAWBACKS Homemade sprays generally won't last as long after they're applied as commercial repellents and might injure your plants in some circumstances, depending on what you put into the spray.

THE BOTTOM LINE I like homemade remedies for repelling deer. They won't always work, and depending on what you're adding to your spray they may burn the leaves a little, but they have all of the things in them that the commercial sprays have with the exception of a good chemical to help them stick to the plants you're spraying. Still, it's likely that you can get a good week or two of control with this stuff depending on the weather.

Motion-detecting sprinklers

One of the most interesting devices I've seen for repelling deer is a motion detector that's hooked up to an automatic sprinkler and sold under the name ScareCrow. When a deer moves within range of the motion detector a sprinkler turns on, ideally chasing the deer away. Though unbiased scientific assessments of this product are wanting, I think this is a great idea to try as long as you're not expecting this device to offer any protection from deer over the winter months.

 This control is reported to work quite well and water is pretty darn nontoxic.

 The neighborhood kids might think that it's a great idea to put on their swimsuits and trip the motion sensor on this thing for a little bit of fun.

THE BOTTOM LINE This product is a great idea, but it won't be effective over the winter in most locations.

Rodent control: The organic choices

Controlling rodents is a lot like controlling deer, except that rodents will go under or through almost anything while deer usually go over. As with deer, the time when your plants are most vulnerable to attack is during the winter when food is scarce. A number of synthetic controls for rodents are available that can be quite effective. Based largely on baits, these controls attract the pest with the promise of food and then kill it with a poison. The weakness of these baits is that the poison is usually pretty toxic to mammals, including humans. We're just not that different from rats and mice physiologically. Organic choices for controlling rodents can be labor intensive, but they don't tend to include the poisons that the synthetics do.

Most of the plentiful organic choices out there for getting rid of rodents include mechanical traps or repellents. Generally the organic choices aren't as effective as poisons, but that doesn't mean that you can't get satisfactory control from them; it's just that it's very difficult to knock out a large population of rabbits by livetrapping or by spraying cayenne pepper around your garden.

Fencing

Fencing to control rodents can work quite well, but unfortunately these guys do dig, and they stretch too, so fencing should be placed in the earth as deep as possible so that the critters can't get underneath it, and it should go as high as possible so that they can't go over it. That set of words "as possible" can lead to some real problems. How deep is deep enough? Should I disturb the roots of plants in the area? How high is high enough? What if branches get caught in the fencing? Furthermore, a variety of different rodents may be trying to make their way through the fence. Woodchucks, gophers, mice, rats, voles, and rabbits all want to get into your garden, and all have different abilities in terms of digging, climbing, and jumping.

The best way to control rodents, as a group, is with a fence that's buried as much as a foot deep in the ground, but stop if you hit the root system of a young tree. Going as high as three and a half or four feet is good, but stop if you run into tree branches. Be sure to customize the fence to suit your needs; for example, a vole will easily get through fences with large holes, and even most small holes, and a rabbit will easily jump over most low fences and dig under fences that aren't well buried. When you choose a fence for rodents, be sure to select a mesh size that won't allow their small bodies to fit through. Chicken wire is usually best as it excludes most rodents, even voles.

 Fencing is a safe way to deter rodents that usually works quite well.

 The worst thing in the world, even worse than having rodents in the first place, is to have rodents get through your fence. And it will happen. And you will be angry.

If it doesn't bother you visually, fencing is a great way to keep critters out, but do realize that despite your best efforts they'll still get inside your fence once in awhile, especially voles. It's one of life's great mysteries that you can ponder as you dig to sink the fence even deeper.

Glue traps

One of the nastier ways for a rodent to go is via a glue trap. Glue traps are a little like sticky cards for mammals; they're basically small pans filled with a substance that won't let go of a rodent once it puts a foot down, keeping the rodent attached to the pan until it expires either from suffocation or starvation. These traps usually don't include any bait, so the rodent must conveniently walk through a trap for it to work.

 These traps tend to be effective at catching the mouse whose habits you know well.

 These traps aren't going to be effective at getting rid of all the rodents you're dealing with. Some rodents will avoid them.

 This is a good if somewhat cruel tool for getting rid of that one mouse that has a set of habits you can predict.

Mechanical traps

Trapping rodents in snap traps or no-kill traps is an option that most gardeners like because they can see the results of their efforts and they can move any animals they catch from one place to another without killing them. Most of these traps function on the same principle, which is that the rodent is attracted to some bait and then is either caught or killed when a mechanism is tripped. As a general rule, the more sensitive the tripping mechanism is the more efficient your trap will be.

Trapping won't rid your property of rodents—there are just too many of them around in most situations for these traps to eradicate the problem—but it certainly can help. Various researchers have found different traps to be effective depending on the season, climate, type of pest, and so forth (Wiener and Smith 1972), so if you're going to use traps, try a few kinds to see which is most effective for you. Remember that the sensitivity of the trap release mechanism is usually the thing that separates the best traps from the others.

BENEFITS Traps allow you to quickly assess how effective your control measures are. If a mouse dies, you'll know it. Live traps also have the advantage of being a so-called humane way to remove small mammals from your property, and snap traps can be quite humane too as long as they break the animal's neck and not its leg.

DRAWBACKS If you don't check your live traps, these sorts of traps aren't very humane. Also, if you're using live traps, you need a place to set the animal free, which may be difficult if you live in a location where it's illegal to transport trapped wild animals off of your property.

THE BOTTOM LINE For most gardeners, livetrapping or snap trapping is a great alternative to poisons, which I'll admit I'm not too fond of. If you're livetrapping, make sure you've got a good spot to release the critters that doesn't include the neighbor's yard (unless that neighbor gave you a Japanese beetle trap for your last birthday).

Repellents

A wide array of repellents is available for squirrels, rabbits, voles, moles, rats, and mice. In general, these repellents work about as well as deer repellents work—that is to say, most of them work quite well as long as other food can be found but cease to be very effective when other food is scarce. As with deer repellents, homemade rodent repellents function about as effectively as commercial repellents except that the commercial repellents tend to last longer.

While some research has shown eggs to effectively repel rodents, they don't tend to be as repellent to voles as they are to deer (Witmer, Hakim, and Moser 2000). Some people have found blood meal to be very effective against rabbits, while others have found it useless. Castor oil, on the other hand, is an easily found commercially available substance that can be repellent to both moles and voles if applied at a high concentration (Dudderar,

Tellman, and Elshoff 1997; Witmer, Hakim, and Moser 2000). Studies have shown that castor oil can work for more than a month against moles (Dudderar, Tellman, and Elshoff 1997), which is a lot longer than most other repellents. You can purchase castor oil and make your own spray, but the commercially available repellents have better directions and are much easier to mix up and apply. I would stay away from homemade castor oil remedies.

BENEFITS Repellents for rodents seem to work well in general. Castor oil in particular seems to be effective and to last longer than would be expected.

DRAWBACKS Repellents don't tend to offer 100 percent control.

THE BOTTOM LINE Repellents for rodents can be pretty effective, so they're certainly worth a shot. I especially like commercial formulations of castor oil.

Rodent control: The synthetic choices

A huge number of synthetic poisons exist for controlling rabbits, rats, moles, voles, and other small critters. The first modern poison to be commonly used was warfarin, an anticoagulant that has to be eaten multiple times before the rodent dies. Due to overuse and a buildup in resistance, warfarin is no longer as effective as it once was; however, plenty of baits still use this poison. Anticoagulant poisons and some others are listed below.

How effective poison baits are at controlling critters depends on two things: how attractive the bait is to the critter and how effective the poison is against the critter. Baits change all the time, so I'm going to leave that part of the equation alone, but I'll take a look at some of the more common poisons used in different baits to control rodents.

Bromadiolone and broadifacoum

Bromadiolone and broadifacoum are considered some of the more advanced anticoagulant poisons that you can buy for rodents and are supposed to kill with only a single feeding. As with warfarin, some rodent populations show resistance to these rodenticides (Meisenheimer et al. 1994). These poisons are usually sold as baits in some kind of enclosure that blocks children and animals from having access.

 These anticoagulant poisons are much more effective than warfarin with fewer resistance issues and kill more rapidly (usually two to four days after feeding).

 Various rodent populations show some resistance to these chemicals. These chemicals are very toxic to humans and other animals.

 Bromadiolone and broadifacoum are very poisonous chemicals that can be effective against rodents if used wisely.

Bromethalin

Bromethalin isn't an anticoagulant poison but rather one that works by affecting the rodent's nervous system. It's an extremely toxic compound with the advantage that it can be used against rodents that are resistant to anticoagulants. Like the other rodent poisons, this one is almost always in an enclosure that prevents animals besides rodents from coming into contact with the poison.

 This is probably the best available poison for anticoagulant-resistant rodents.

 This is a potent poison and as such is toxic to humans and other animals.

Bromethalin is one of the best rodent poisons available and is particularly useful for anticoagulant-resistant pests. This is a potent poison and great care should be taken with its use.

Cholecalciferol

Cholecalciferol (vitamin D_3) is a compound that occurs naturally in humans and other animals, including rodents. When it's purchased by a consumer as a vitamin supplement, or as a poison for rodents, it's usually produced synthetically using various chemical processes. This chemical works by causing calcium from the animal's bones to enter the blood, leading to what is essentially calcium poisoning. Although it's a vitamin, this compound can be extremely toxic if too much of it is ingested. As always, the dose makes the poison.

BENEFITS This chemical is considered somewhat safer than most of the other rodent poisons you could use. Additionally, rodents that are resistant to anticoagulants should still be susceptible to this.

DRAWBACKS This chemical isn't completely innocuous, despite the fact that it's a vitamin we need in our bodies.

THE BOTTOM LINE This is far from the most common poison you're going to see on garden center shelves, but it can be quite effective, especially against rodent populations that are resistant to the more popular anticoagulants.

Warfarin

Warfarin, released in 1950, is one of the oldest of the anticoagulant rodenticides and can still be found in many rodent poisons today. It acts by preventing the rodent's blood from clotting and can also cause capillaries to burst, essentially causing the afflicted rodent to bleed to death internally. Warfarin is one of the safer rodenticides (though still far from safe!) because it usually needs to be ingested many times in order to work. While that means that rodents thus poisoned don't die as quickly as some gardeners would like them to, it also means that accidental ingestion, while quite serious, isn't as serious as accidental ingestion of other rodent killers. One of the biggest problems with this chemical is that rodents show some resistance to it (Quy et al. 1995), so it may not be effective at all if you happen to have a population of warfarin-resistant rodents around.

Warfarin can be effective against nonresistant rodent populations.

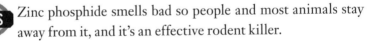 It usually takes multiple feedings to kill the rodents, so the control isn't immediate. Resistant populations of rodents, particularly rats, do exist.

 Warfarin's day as a rodenticide is probably almost done because of resistance problems and because other, faster-acting poisons are available.

Zinc phosphide

Zinc phosphide is a particularly nasty poison that smells like garlic. This strong scent is a good thing because it keeps humans away, but it apparently doesn't repel rodents. Phosphorus poisons such as this one work by causing the animal's liver, kidneys, and heart to disintegrate. Zinc phosphide also makes rats attempt to vomit, a bodily function they're incapable of. This poison is toxic to birds, humans, dogs, and most other mammals, so needs to be used with the greatest care.

 Zinc phosphide smells bad so people and most animals stay away from it, and it's an effective rodent killer.

DRAWBACKS This is a very toxic poison.

THE BOTTOM LINE Zinc phosphide is an effective poison that's very toxic.

Slug and snail control: The organic choices

I practically never use poisons on slugs, only deterrents. I've found that it just isn't worth killing slugs; it's better by far to chase them away, because if you deter slugs from eating your valuable plants, such as your hostas, they'll actually feed on certain weeds plants (though they do seem to like tomatoes and hostas best, when they can get their grubby foot on them).

All kinds of organic slug remedies are available, most of which are relatively safe for the environment. The organic controls available for slugs are models of the positive traits that we associate with organic growing.

Diatomaceous earth

Right off the garden center shelf, diatomaceous earth is one of the best methods of keeping slugs away from your plants. As mentioned in the chapter on insect control, diatomaceous earth is a very fine dust that's composed of the skeletons of diatoms, which are made of silicon and are very sharp. As a snail or slug tries to cross over this substance it gets microscopic cuts that may or may not kill it, but either way, slugs hate crossing over this stuff.

 Diatomaceous earth is very effective at stopping slugs in their tracks and is relatively safe as long as it isn't inhaled.

 This product isn't as effective when it's wet and doesn't provide the satisfaction that some people feel from poisoning slugs. Diatomaceous earth is dangerous if it's inhaled. Wearing a respirator when applying this material is a good idea.

I like diatomaceous earth for controlling slugs a lot. It's effective and relatively safe as long as you don't inhale it.

Homemade remedies

There are numerous homemade remedies for controlling slugs and snails, more than for any other single pest that I know of with the possible exception of deer. Most of these homemade remedies involve creating some kind of a barrier that slugs can't cross, much like diatomaceous earth. I've tried many of the various homemade barrier materials against slugs, including used coffee grounds, ashes, eggshells, tobacco, and copper, and have found that the only one that really provides any reliable protection is tobacco. The other barriers tend to allow slugs to walk right over them with barely a shrug. It's worth noting, though, that mixing 20 percent chewing tobacco with 80 percent used coffee grounds is quite effective at repelling slugs and will, in fact, kill slugs that linger too long.

Though tobacco looks good at first glance, some caveats make it less attractive when you investigate more deeply. If you're growing tomatoes, potatoes, or other crops that might get tobacco mosaic virus, you might prefer to avoid this particular remedy. Additionally, dogs and cats sometimes eat the tobacco, which may poison them. As indicated in the section on using nicotine against insects, tobacco can't be used in commercial organic growing, only in organic gardening at home.

Homemade beer traps are a splendid method for attracting slugs and work quite effectively when properly prepared. Place a container like a pie tin or margarine tub in the ground with the lip of the container level with the soil surrounding it, then add beer until it's about an inch short of the top. This trap will attract slugs and snails and will result in their falling into the beer and drowning.

Since I started writing and speaking about homemade slug controls, a number of people have told me about pouring salt over slugs to kill them. Yes, pouring salt over a slug will kill it, but in my experience, for every one slug you find in an area, ten more are waiting for you to go away, so I'm not big on this remedy. I just don't think that you can kill enough to make much of a difference using this method; besides, salt isn't good for most of your plants.

BENEFITS I find homemade slug controls tremendously fun to try, whether or not they actually work. Beer traps are a tried-and-true method, and if the trap can be filled with only half a beer, so much the better. Deterrents based on chewing tobacco definitely work, though periods of rain may decrease their effectiveness.

DRAWBACKS Many of the homemade deterrents that I try out just don't work that well, with the exception of tobacco, which has some major problems and shouldn't be used for organic production.

THE BOTTOM LINE Beer traps are definitely a keeper, but once you get beyond that few remedies are both effective and reasonably safe.

Iron phosphate

One of the great success stories in organic slug and snail control is iron phosphate. This simple compound when eaten by slugs inhibits their ability to feed. Not eating won't kill the slug very quickly, but given a few days the slug will indeed die. Iron phosphate is generally applied as a bait, so it's usually formulated with food items that the slug will find attractive. This chemical doesn't break down nearly as rapidly as synthetic slug poisons do, making it a longer-lasting form of control.

In tests where iron phosphate has been compared with metaldehyde, the standard for slug killers, it hasn't been as effective at killing slugs (Speiser and Kistler 2001), but it has certainly been much more effective than nothing. Tests in Hawaii found that orchid-eating snails were generally not attracted to the bait (Hollingsworth and Armstrong 2003), but there are many different types of baits, so don't be discouraged by this one failure. Realize that different baits will be attractive to different creatures.

BENEFITS Iron phosphate is a relatively safe poison that's effective on slugs. Metaldehyde, the most common synthetic choice for slugs, has some significant drawbacks that may make iron phosphate especially attractive in situations where animals or children might come into contact with the bait.

DRAWBACKS Iron phosphate may not be quite as effective as synthetic poisons on slugs.

THE BOTTOM LINE Iron phosphate is safer than the synthetic options, though it may be somewhat less effective. All in all I would say that this pesticide is a keeper. I'm willing to live with a few slugs if it means that I don't have to deal with metaldehyde, which has effects on dogs and other animals that I'm not willing to risk.

Yucca extract

Sprays are available commercially that contain extract from yucca plants, which is supposed to repel snails and slugs and prevent them from feeding on plants. A test comparing a variety of different poisons and repellents on their ability to keep snails away from orchid roots showed that yucca extract works, although metaldehyde and methiocarb proved to be more effective in the same test (Hollingsworth and Armstrong 2003).

 Yucca extracts do repel some types of snails and are relatively safe.

DRAWBACKS A limited amount of research has been done on these extracts and though I would expect them to consistently repel many types of snails and slugs, it's difficult to assess exactly how repellent they are without more research. Yucca extracts probably need to be reapplied every week or two, especially if there are heavy rains.

THE BOTTOM LINE Yucca extracts are a neat idea, but the presence of an effective and safe poison, iron phosphate, makes these extracts of questionable value.

Slug and snail control: The synthetic choices

Many of the past sections have compared the dangers of organic compounds with those of synthetic compounds and concluded that both can be quite dangerous. The case with slugs is a little different. The synthetic pesticides here certainly have their advantages, but in terms of danger the organic methods seem quite a bit safer. Still, I would hesitate to call anything that's intended to kill something completely safe.

Metaldehyde

Metaldehyde, once used as a camp stove fuel, has been the standard for slug killers since it was discovered that it was effective at killing slugs in the 1930s. Metaldehyde is a poison that destroys the mucus-producing membrane of slugs (Triebskorn, Christensen, and Heim 1998), causing them to dry out. Some people have noted that since metaldehyde poisoning dries them out, perhaps if the poisoned slugs were in wet conditions they could survive, but this isn't the case at all. Once a mucus membrane is destroyed, it's destroyed for good. This poison is usually prepared as a bait—that is, mixed with things that are attractive to slugs and then placed near the plant that needs to be protected. Incorporation in baits tends to prevent chemicals from breaking down in the sun, giving them a longer residual activity against pests, but metaldehyde is sensitive to light and won't be effective for as long if exposed to sunlight.

Metaldehyde is a tremendously effective poison against slugs and will do the job for you where you need to clear out a slug population. Unfortunately, metaldehyde is dangerous to mammals, including humans, if it gets into their digestive tract. For humans this isn't usually a concern because adults generally don't eat things that are labeled as pesticides and they have the common sense to keep their children away from such, but the same can't be said for dogs, birds, and other animals who may find metaldehyde baits tasty, leading to potentially fatal poisoning.

 BENEFITS This is a particularly effective poison that will control slugs and snails in most situations.

DRAWBACKS This pesticide is toxic to many animals, and especially to dogs that may find this compound attractive. This is not a pesticide to be applied willy-nilly across a garden.

THE BOTTOM LINE Metaldehyde is an effective way to control slugs and snails as long as there aren't any animals in the area that you're fearful of poisoning. If animal poisoning is a concern, deterrents or iron phosphate is almost certainly a better choice for you.

Methiocarb and carbaryl

Numerous snail and slug baits include the carbamate poisons carbaryl or methiocarb, which you may recognize from the insecticide chapter as nerve poisons that have been available for many years. These poisons are quite effective against snails and slugs and are often used alone or in conjunction with metaldehyde in slug and snail baits. The information provided on the toxicity of these compounds in the insecticides chapter applies here, but it's worth noting that when formulated as bait rather than as a spray, these poisons last longer.

 BENEFITS These poisons, especially in combination with metaldehyde, are quite effective at killing slugs and snails.

DRAWBACKS These carbamate poisons, though somewhat safer than many other pesticides, are nerve toxins. Compounding this problem, whenever these poisons are formulated with metaldehyde, all of the detriments of metaldehyde come along for the ride.

THE BOTTOM LINE Methiocarb and carbaryl are valuable compounds for clearing out slug populations but are probably more than most gardeners need. Because of the problems with metaldehyde and because slug killers containing these compounds are often formulated with it, I tend to shy away from them.

THE BEST CHOICES FOR YOU

When it comes to controlling birds, deer, rodents, and mollusks, there's a very clear distinction between organic and synthetic choices. The organic methods are simply safer than the synthetic ones. For the control of birds and rodents in particular, my opinion is that the synthetic poisons that can be used are too toxic for most situations. I personally would prefer to use the organic choices in almost every case.

8
Organic Practices and Our Ecosystem

Are organic growing and gardening really good for our ecosystem? Can our planet flourish as a result of everyone turning to organics for their food instead of eating conventionally grown produce? As people look more and more deeply into the use of organic techniques I think most of them, including knowledgeable organic proponents, come to the same conclusion: Organic gardening and growing don't currently have all of the answers to the world's problems, or even to all of the problems in your garden, but they're a really good place to start.

When the organic movement began way back in the early 1900s its focus was on the quality of land and how we could work to keep this land and the plants that live in it healthy. This included recycling organic matter by adding compost, and even reusing animal and human waste as fertilizers. These practices kept soils fertile and plants healthy, and as a consequence reduced the need for pesticides and for shipping in offsite fertilizers (such as Peruvian guano and Chilean nitrates, which are today considered organic fertilizers).

Because of the advent of synthetic fertilizers, which made everything seem easy, practices that built up organic matter in the soil were underused for a few decades, but today most farmers worth their salt understand that incorporating organic matter into their land is a very important part of maintaining the fertility of our earth. Using organic matter to revitalize soil is the most basic and important part of organic growing and gardening. If we remember this and follow it, we're ensuring a better future for our gardens.

Environmental benefits

Organic growing, when done properly, is extremely beneficial to the land on which a garden or farm sits as well as to the land around it. It reduces the amount of input that needs to be supplied, while improving the ability of the land to support plant life over the long term and making you feel good about the way you treat your land.

Organic matter

Organic gardening practices can make a piece of ground a fertile place for your plants for years to come if you treat this piece of ground with care. As I've emphasized throughout this book, the heart and soul of organic gardening is supplying the ground with organic materials such as compost to make your earth a healthier place. Practices such as using green manure, composting, and mulching reinvigorate the land by returning nutrients to it and making it more capable of sustaining plant life, not only now but for years into the future. People talk about good, rich top-soil and how great it is to see this type of earth when they till or dig in their gardens. Well, this type of soil comes from a buildup of organic materials over time on a spot of ground. If crops are constantly being harvested and removed and organic material is never returned to the soil, this beautiful topsoil will slowly leave your property. It's only through using organic techniques that we can maintain good healthy soil for our children to enjoy in the future.

Pest controls

As is probably obvious from the past few chapters, I'm not fond of many of the pesticides that organic growers use to control pests. That doesn't mean, however, that I don't like organic pest control techniques. On the contrary, those techniques that involve a reduction in pesticide use such as intercropping and using resistant species are absolutely essential to gardening success. Those organic techniques that help to reduce the use of pesticides are an important part of keeping our planet free from all sorts of chemicals.

In various spots this book has defended the safety of some synthetic pesticides; however, there's little doubt that certain other synthetic pesticides have the potential to seriously damage our planet. Through using already known organic techniques and discovering new ones we can minimize the use of pesticides, both synthetic and organic, and thereby protect our planet from the dangers that these chemicals present.

We, as a society, need to be concerned about our use of pesticides. The environmental effects that certain pesticides can have when they're misapplied, or even when they're applied correctly, can be sobering. For example, applications of broad-spectrum insecticides such as permethrin, carbaryl, rotenone, and pyrethrum to plants will kill beneficial insects as well as pests. In fact, it's practically impossible to avoid this result if you're using these types of broad-spectrum insecticides. Applications of fungicides can affect the beneficial mycorrhizal fungi that surround your plants' roots and help them to take up nutrients. Applications of preemergence herbicides such as trifluralin can affect the growth of your plants' roots. Repeated applications of copper and sulfur can cause a buildup of these elements in the soil and make it less able to sustain plant life. Wow, that's quite a list—and we haven't even started to look at problems that can occur if pesticides are misapplied! Fortunately for us, while the problems that I just listed are real, they also tend to be temporary and if you only apply pesticides once in a long while (once or twice a year) these effects are unlikely to result in long-lasting problems.

When use of pesticides isn't minimized, or applications are made to inappropriate areas, effects on the environment can be terrible. Pesticides used in this way have the potential to affect wildlife, soil-dwelling organisms, and water sources such as ponds and groundwater. Commercial applications of rotenone, glyphosate, pyrethrum, and many other chemicals can kill frogs, fish, and other creatures in streams and ponds. Many of the chemicals we use are poisonous to animals, so if we apply them to a place where animals may go, poisoning is a distinct possibility. Application of pesticides on windy days leads to problems because these pesticides will drift from the area where they're applied to other areas that might be hurt by the pesticide. For example, if a lawn care company comes out to your property and sprays 2,4-D on the grass to control your dandelions and it's a windy day, it's possible that the wind will blow that pesticide right up into your trees, which could cause them to become quite sick.

On a grander scale, the application of pesticides to agricultural land over the years has raised a number of environmental issues. Certain pesticides can build up in the environment and though they may not cause overt sickness (such as cancer) or death, they may cause more insidious problems. Perhaps the most significant research I've seen that influences my feelings about pesticide application is work that looks at how pesticides can mimic natural hormones. Research conducted by Peter Vonier and cooperators (1996) shows that certain pesticides (such as the now-banned DDT), if present in combination with other pesticides and at a high enough concentration, can affect the reproductive systems of wildlife, particularly alligators. I should note that these researchers were working primarily with substances that are no longer available, but this study still provides food for thought.

Another serious finding concerning pesticide application at a grander scale comes from research conducted by Tyrone Hayes at the University of California at Berkeley. Dr. Hayes has experimented with a number of pesticides, most notably atrazine, and found that it has estrogenic effects on animals, specifically frogs. In fact, frogs exposed to this chemical during their development may well develop both ovaries and testes (Hayes et al. 2002). This is especially significant since atrazine is one of the most commonly used herbicides in the world at the time of this writing.

What it all comes down to for me is that we must find ways to reduce pesticide use, and if a particular pesticide shows itself to be potentially harmful to the environment, we should do away with it as quickly as possible. Organic practices don't necessarily have all of the answers for reducing pesticides, but those who practice organic techniques at least have the right mindset, and that mindset is what's needed if a change is to happen.

Environmental drawbacks

As you've probably gleaned from the past few chapters, organic growing is not risk free. While it seems intuitive that conventional growing and synthetic pesticides are more detrimental to the ecosystem than organic, this isn't necessarily true in every situation. Organic growing can have effects on our ecosystem that are different from, or in some cases surprisingly similar to, conventional growing but that are no less real. In this section we're going to take a look at potential effects of organic production practices on the environment, while also noting some of the effects on the environment that synthetic or conventional practices could have.

Pesticides

Most of the problems with organic growing involve the use of organic pesticides. If you don't and never plan to use organic pesticides, this isn't an issue you need to concern yourself with, and if you're using synthetic chemicals you're probably well aware of the risks, but for the rest of us it should be one of the first things we consider when making decisions about whether we want to go organic. Most organic pesticides that have been examined extensively have relatively few effects on humans at low doses, but then low doses of synthetic chemicals also tend to have few effects on humans. There's a certain amount of hypocrisy on the part of our government here, because the requirements to test synthetic chemicals in order to insure safety are extremely stringent but the same requirements aren't in place for natural compounds; and although natural things can certainly be banned (such as marijuana), natural pesticides are exempt from some of the rigorous testing that synthetic chemicals must undergo, such as mandatory testing for pesticide residues. This raises an important question: Are we trying to protect people and our environment from dangerous pesticides in general or just those we make ourselves?

Those who make the rules (the U.S. Environmental Protection Agency) point out that most of the natural poisons we use as pesticides are things that we, or other people, are likely to come into contact with regardless of whether we spray a pesticide or not, but they fail to recognize that the dose makes the poison, which, by the way, is the title of a book by Alice Ottoboni (1997) that I've mentioned previously and will again recommend. Almost anything can be poisonous at a high enough dose and almost anything is safe at a low enough dose. It's convenient to say that because a chemical is natural we can't avoid it anyway, but really, how many of us will have the opportunity to rub up against the tree from which neem is derived, against the derris plant from which rotenone is derived, or against the type of chrysanthemum from which pyrethrum is derived? And even if you did have the opportunity to rub up against them, would you encounter the same amount of these chemicals as when you spray them on your plants? The answer is no.

The U.S. Environmental Protection Agency (1996) has written guidelines for the testing of microbial and other natural pesticides that ensure "to the greatest extent possible, that only the minimum data sufficient to make scientifically sound regulatory decisions will be required." I'm sure that many of us would like to see more than the minimum required, especially when the minimum doesn't typically include residue testing—testing of the residue that may well be on our food.

What if we didn't know that a particular naturally derived toxin was carcinogenic and decided to test it on insects and found out that, lo and behold, it killed insects? Because that toxin was natural, it could go through a faster and easier screening process than that for synthetic compounds. Can you imagine the problems that might occur after five, ten, or twenty years? And it all could have been avoided if only the natural compound had gone through the same sort of screening process that's required of all synthetic compounds. This doesn't present a pretty picture. Is it likely to happen? No. But what you have to ask yourself is whether it's a risk you're comfortable with.

Though human toxicity and carcinogenicity are certainly important issues, easily the most overlooked problem with organic pesticides is their toxicity to creatures in the environment. Many of the synthetic pesticides we use today are undoubtedly toxic to a wide range of organisms, but some people seem to think that organic pesticides are less detrimental. This is far from the truth. As you read in the chapter on insecticides, natural pesticides such as rotenone and pyrethrum are actually quite toxic to various organisms, especially aquatic creatures. In fact, rotenone is one of the most effective fish poisons available today. Just because this chemical is sold as an insecticide doesn't make it any less dangerous to fish.

Compounding the problem of their lethality to a wide range of animals is the fact that although many organic pesticides break down relatively quickly, a number are based on elements—including copper and sulfur—that don't break down and can sit in the soil for many years affecting the growth and health of future crops. The use of these pesticides needs to be consciously minimized, just like synthetic pesticides, to reduce the potential for environmental damage.

Fertilizers

Though I'm generally a proponent of organic fertilizers, these products do have some significant environmental drawbacks, just like synthetic fertilizers. First of all, let's face the fact that not all organic fertilizers are perfectly renewable. Organic fertilizers such as rock phosphate, potassium minerals, and guanos are mined and so are limited resources. Indeed, we've already drastically affected the world's supply of guano by mining it so heavily from South America in the nineteenth century that it's no longer an inexpensive nitrogen supply for our crops. Fertilizers such as alfalfa meal, seaweed extracts, bonemeal, and, of course, composted manures are all much more renewable though not as filled with concentrated nutrients.

Organic fertilizers tend to have lower concentrations of nutrients in them than synthetic fertilizers, so to apply a given amount of nutrition to the ground more of the organic fertilizer is needed, meaning more lifting and carrying. These fertilizers also tend to be more expensive than synthetic fertilizers (unless you're doing your own composting) because a larger amount of these fertilizers is needed to get the same amount of nutrition as would be found in a smaller quantity of synthetic.

A myth exists that the nutrients in organic fertilizers won't leach or run off and contaminate nearby bodies of water. This is completely false. The nutrients in any organic fertilizer can leave a site via water movement, such as leaching through the ground or washing away with rain, and can contaminate streams, lakes, and even groundwater. The word *eutrophication* refers to the process of overaddition of nutrients to a body of water and the resulting increased growth of algae and reduced oxygen in the water. Eutrophication is often blamed on synthetic fertilizers rather than organic, and to some extent that makes sense since synthetic fertilizers are applied more often than organic fertilizers. However, organic fertilizers are just as likely to cause this process to occur as synthetic fertilizers if they're used in the overaggressive way that many people fertilize their lawns.

What to do?

Is organic gardening really better for the environment? Yes, no question about it, it's better for the environment. However, that answer isn't without a few caveats. The basics tenets of organic gardening include reusing organic materials and avoiding pesticides. Just by following these simple rules your garden will grow and flourish in harmony with nature. Sure, you'll have more weeds, and you'll certainly have your share of insect and disease problems too, but you'll also have the satisfaction of knowing that you're not polluting the environment.

Once you start adding pesticides, even though they may come from natural sources, you start messing with a natural system and could throw your garden out of whack. Poisons beget poisons—in other words, once you start using pesticides, particularly insecticides, you'll get rid of many of the beneficial insects in your garden. Once these are gone pest insects will flourish because they'll rebound faster than beneficial insects and you'll end up having to reapply insecticides in order to keep the pests at bay. The more you apply pesticides, the greater the danger is that you'll have a negative impact on your garden or yourself. Not only are organic pesticides not immune from this vicious cycle, they can be some of the worst offenders. Insecticides like rotenone and pyrethrum will take a heavy toll on beneficial insects and often result in the need to reapply pesticides. Other organic pesticides such as those containing copper, sulfur, and other elements can build up in the soil and cause long-term problems. Both organic and synthetic fertilizers also result in problems if they're overused.

Where does it all end? That's your decision, but here's my two cents' worth: I think that we, as gardeners, need to reduce our pesticide and fertilizer use drastically. Does that mean that I think we should eliminate them? No, certainly not, at least not until we get something better. In extremely hard times they can be a tremendous help. But we've been encouraged by our neighbors and by highly paid marketing firms that work for chemical companies to have perfect lawns and gardens with nary a weed nor insect. This kind of garden is not only unnatural, it's unsustainable and it runs the risk of damaging the environment from pesticide and fertilizer overuse. Consider the long-term consequences of the things you add to your garden and apply chemicals judiciously. If you don't, we'll all pay the price in the long term.

9

The Question of Organic Food

At this point, if you've been reading straight through this book instead of jumping around, you've got a pretty good handle on many of the methods that organic gardeners and growers may use to control pests. Because we regulate what goes on and into the food that comes out of our own gardens, we tend to be pretty confident about its quality. Food from the grocery store is different, though. On the shelves of almost every major grocery store are foods labeled as organically grown. This distinction indicates that the food was grown in accordance with the USDA's organic growing standards or might even comply with the standards of other certifying agencies that are even more stringent than the USDA. Over the years numerous claims have been made regarding the quality of organic food, claims ranging from reduced concentration of pesticides to increased nutritional value.

Some people believe firmly in the benefits of organic food, and some dismiss these benefits as hype. This is a hot-button issue with two sides who aren't particularly friendly to each other and who refuse to play nice. The organic side uses propaganda to instill fear out of proportion with the actual danger of conventionally grown products in order to promote sales, while the other side refuses to see potential benefits of alternative growing systems. Is it any wonder that you can't get a straight answer from these people as to how safe organic foods are? This chapter takes a look at organically grown fruits and vegetables and examines why they might or might not be better than those produced conventionally.

When children fight they like to lay the blame on the other child by saying that the other one started it. This provides quite a conundrum for the person who has to break up the children, because there's often no reasonable way to determine who's telling the truth, and furthermore, one child may reason that the other started the fight because of some harsh words while the other child may consider the first child to have started the fight because that child took the first swing. The truth is, of course, that both children contributed to the fight, and while it can be argued that one deserves a harsher punishment than the other, there can be little doubt that neither of the children deserves a lollipop for his or her actions. In terms of the name-calling between those who believe that organically grown food is better for you than conventionally grown food and those who believe the opposite, a similar situation exists. The first stone was thrown (and I think we're all glad it was thrown!) by people who questioned the safety of growing plants with synthetic fertilizers and pesticides. J. I. Rodale and Rachel Carson were two of these people and the work they presented in their writings did indeed show that some pesticides, especially when used incorrectly, can prove quite damaging to people and the environment. Largely because of the work of people like these, pesticides are now subjected to much more rigorous testing than was the case only twenty years ago, and incredibly more than was the case sixty years ago.

During the time that the government was working out and fine-tuning the processes involved in testing pesticides to make sure that they're safe (a process still going on today), some creative and well-intentioned people cashed in on the public's fears by growing food items for sale without synthetic pesticides—an excellent marketing gambit by all accounts. As testing became better and our conventional pest control practices became safer, the advertising that organic producers used didn't let up much, which makes perfect sense if you rely on the public's fear of a particular product to lead them to buy yours. It's difficult to call the practice dishonest, because most organic producers choose to remain blissfully unaware of the goings-on in the synthetic pesticide world.

The propaganda that organic producers offer the world includes a variety of claims, some obviously true, such as the claim that organic production helps to preserve the soil, and some that are more questionable, such as the claim that polluting chemicals aren't used in organic agriculture. But the claim that drives me crazy is that organic food is pesticide free. This claim is so obviously untrue it makes my hair stand on end. When the point is made that natural pesticides are pesticides too, organic proponents frequently retort that organic pesticides degrade quickly and will never affect the environment and certainly can't be found as residue on food. This statement is simply not true.

If you've read this far, you probably think that I'm coming down kind of hard on the organic producers, and maybe I am. But just because I took a look at them first doesn't mean that I agree with them any more or less than I agree with their opponents. Antiorganic activists have been around a long time and will continue to be around far into the future. Over the years they've presented a myriad of reasonable arguments against organic growing, such as the fact that organic producers use poisons too, as well as some less-than-reasonable arguments, such as the questionable statement that organic production isn't better for the land. Why can't we all just accept that different people have different opinions and different priorities, make a concerted effort to get the facts out so that the average person can make a rational decision about what sort of food to buy, and do away with all of the muck? Actually, I think I can answer that. Conflict, even when it's based on questionable facts and rhetoric, is good for business. What a sad state of affairs.

Pesticide residues

A big reason—in fact, *the* reason—to choose organically over conventionally grown food is a pronounced reduction in the amounts of synthetic pesticide residues on organic food. Some organic bashers have suggested that synthetic pesticide residues get onto organically grown produce, and some undoubtedly do, but when research has investigated this it has generally found fewer synthetic pesticide residues on organically than conventionally grown crops. A review of some of the more important articles addressing the amount of synthetic pesticide residues on food produced organically, conventionally, and with IPM (integrated pest management; more on this in a minute) conducted by Brian Baker and others from the Organic Materials Review Institute (2002) showed that, indeed, food produced using organic methods had fewer residues of synthetic pesticides. This review, unfortunately, didn't look at residues of organic pesticides, which, one would expect, would be higher in organically produced food. In fact, this review actually pointed out that there's "a lack of analytical methods for residues" of organic pesticides.

Indeed, it wasn't until 1998 that a method of collectively testing for the residues of the most common organic insecticides was published (Zang 1998), and although this methodology is relatively straightforward, I don't know of a single study that uses it to establish the amount of organic pesticide residues on various food items. Other methods for testing individual organic pesticides have been around since the 1980s and these have shown that residues of rotenone and its degradation product rotenolone can last on food for at least two weeks (Newsome and Shields 1980) and probably significantly longer if environmental conditions aren't conducive to pesticide breakdown. Tests on fruit samples conducted in the early 1980s also demonstrated that pyrethrin (one of the constituents of pyrethrum), though an organic pesticide reported to break down quickly, was present on oranges, pears, and plums that were tested for its presence (Ryan, Pilon, and Leduc 1982).

A common belief among people who eat organic food but who've had no experience growing this food commercially is that pesticides are never, or at least only rarely, used on these foods. These people usually understand that particular pesticides *can* be used but think that these pesticides *won't* be used under most circumstances. This is a misconception that needs a little bit of clearing up. First of all, organic producers usually are very hesitant to apply pesticides unless they have to, but then so are producers who use synthetic chemicals. These things cost money and spraying pesticides isn't cheap. If growers don't have to apply a chemical, they won't. Second, even organic growers can decide to apply pesticides before seeing pests. For many pests, producers can watch the population growing and not apply any chemicals until the pest reaches a specific concentration, but for certain other pests, mostly diseases like scab and fire blight in apples, it makes much more sense to apply chemicals before seeing the pest. That means that certain pesticides are used by organic growers whether or not they see the pest, and while it's true that they probably only apply these chemicals because they have to in order to produce a satisfactory crop, it's a mistake to believe that they're applying pesticides only when they observe pest activity.

Lists out there published primarily by producers of organic foods show the crops that are most likely to be treated with pesticides. These lists usually include apples, pears, and peaches, among others. The lists are intended to demonstrate to the consumer that the foods listed are best not purchased unless they've been organically grown. But in fact, the same foods that conventional producers must apply more pesticides to must also be treated with more pesticides, albeit organic ones, by producers using organic methods. Just because we say that we'll be growing a plant organically doesn't mean that insects and diseases leave the party. Sure, organic producers use more earth-friendly methods such as traps and baits, but these methods are unlikely to completely eliminate the problem by themselves. In fact, when looking at apple orchards, Joseph Kovach and his co-operators at Cornell University found that because of the modest efficacy and short residual activity of most of the organic pesticides, frequent reapplications of these chemicals are often necessary, leading to environmental consequences that may be worse than if conventional pesticides were applied (Kovach et al. 1992).

In all fairness, Dr. Kovach also showed that judicious use of conventional pesticides using a system called IPM (integrated pest management) had less potential for damage than either the simple conventional or organic choices. Even crops sprayed judiciously with pesticides will still retain some of these pesticides when they're harvested and sold, but they're likely to have less synthetic pesticide residues than a similar crop grown without using IPM (Baker 2002) and are likely not to have been sprayed heavily with organic pesticides. It's too bad that the government doesn't have a system for labeling food produced through the use of IPM. In my opinion that would be more valuable than the current system of labeling food as USDA Organic.

Taken as a whole, the available information points to the inescapable conclusion that it's highly likely that organic produce, and especially organic produce from plant species that need to be sprayed a lot in conventional production systems, contains residues of organic pesticides that may be just as harmful as their synthetic cousins, or, as in the case of some toxins like rotenone, perhaps even more so. Once we realize that pesticide residues of one sort or another are probably on at least some of our food, the question then becomes how dangerous these residues actually are to us—and the answer, unfortunately, is that nobody knows.

There's a common perception among the population in general that pesticides cause cancer. This perception is so prevalent that I often see books and magazine articles that simply take it as fact that these products are carcinogens and that don't offer any citation or evidence to support the claim. The problem with this "known fact" is that it comes largely from research that investigates the effects of these chemicals when they're fed to rodents repeatedly over the course of weeks or months using the maximum dose that the rodents can ingest without showing readily apparent signs of poisoning. Under these conditions about 50 percent of chemicals, be they natural or synthetic, end up looking like carcinogens (Ames and Gold 2000). In fact, if we were to base the carcinogenicity of compounds on these tests alone, we would have to ban coffee. Drinking a single cup of coffee, you'll ingest about the same amount of known carcinogens as you would of "carcinogenic" (again based on the rodent tests) synthetic chemicals if you ate produce from the grocery store over the course of a year. And this would be despite the fact that only about 3 percent of the natural substances in coffee have even been tested for their carcinogenicity (Gold et al. 1992). In short, the tests that we base carcinogenicity on aren't reasonable indicators of how carcinogenic pesticides are at the level at which we're likely to ingest them as a consumer, or even as an applicator.

But that's not to say that there aren't studies that point to pesticides as potential carcinogens, because there are. Commonly called epidemiological studies, these investigations follow people who have been exposed to pesticides over time and compare the health of these groups to the health of groups that haven't been exposed to pesticides. Though these studies are generally very informative they do have some pronounced weaknesses, the biggest of which is that people who might be more prone to use pesticides might also be more prone to other activities that may increase or decrease the risk for cancer, such as eating a balanced diet or being exposed to the sun. Nonetheless, these studies provide the best data we currently have on whether exposure to pesticides can cause health problems. Many factors are involved in the development of cancer; pesticide exposure is surely one of them, but the belief that because you were exposed to pesticides you'll develop cancer is an oversimplification of the facts and has little scientific merit.

Studies that have investigated groups of people who are chronically exposed to pesticides, such as farmers and professional pesticide applicators, reveal a cloudy picture. One of the few large studies available (Colt et al. 2001), which investigated more than twenty-six thousand migrant and seasonal farm workers, found that this group, which had regular exposure to pesticides, actually had reduced mortality from cancer when compared to the population at large. In this study particular cancers, including cancers of the buccal cavity, larynx, esophagus, stomach, and skin were higher than normal in those exposed to pesticides; however, cancers of the colon, breast, kidney, pancreas, and lymphohematopoietic system were present in reduced numbers.

Studies of particular cancers that researchers suspect might be somehow related to pesticide use, such as cancer of the prostate, have indeed found links between pesticide use and cancer, but these links have generally been weak (Maele-Fabry and Willems 2003). The occurrence of non-Hodgkin's lymphoma in those exposed to pesticides has been a favorite study topic among epidemiologists, and indeed, an investigation of children demonstrated at least a possibility that exposure to pesticides might increase the chance of this cancer among children (Buckley et al. 2000). Other studies have also shown slight increases in the chances of non-Hodgkin's lymphoma for people exposed to pesticides (Cantor et al. 1992; Zahm and Blair 1992).

All of these studies can cause concern because it's obvious from them that the incidence of specific types of cancer may increase, albeit only slightly, with increased exposure to pesticides. However, a closer look suggests that the people who developed cancer in these studies were exposed to amounts of pesticide well beyond what would be applied by the typical homeowner or gardener. Furthermore, these studies make no distinction between organic and synthetic pesticides. I think of it this way: If we accept the fact that repeatedly exposing rats to high doses of organic or synthetic poisons leads to cancer, doesn't it make sense that repeatedly exposing humans to the same thing is a terrible idea?

We should all be opposed to using unnecessarily large or frequent applications of pesticides, be they organic or synthetic, in any garden or growing situation. In truth, gardeners face very few situations where they *need* to apply a pesticide, especially if other methods of pest control are used. Growers, who depend on their crops for their livelihood, are a different story. If they lose their crops, they lose their livelihood. Certainly the pesticides we use are poisons, but in the quantities found on food, especially if we clean it before we eat it, we just don't have any reason to believe that they'll cause problems. Washing fruits and vegetables, especially with hot water, can significantly reduce the amount of pesticides on them and is a good idea for anyone concerned about residues (Holland et al. 1994).

A much greater problem than that of pesticide contamination would occur if people avoided fruits and vegetables in order to avoid pesticides. High consumption of these nutritious foods (regardless of whether they're produced with organic or synthetic pesticides) is associated with reductions in the occurrences of many diseases, including cancer and cardiovascular disease, while more than two hundred studies have shown diets low in these foods to be associated with a higher incidence of cancer (Ames and Gold 2000).

No study I've ever seen has investigated the health of people who are chronically exposed to organic pesticides, although it's a mistake to assume that in any study investigating pesticide use, the only pesticides that the people were exposed to were synthetic.

Nutrition

Fruits, vegetables, and other foods that are grown organically are usually touted as being more nutritious than similar foods grown conventionally. I'll tell you right now that more nutritious or not, these foods often do taste a heck of a lot better than foods grown conventionally simply because they're usually grown locally, meaning that they can ripen on the plant before being picked. Locally grown food is one of life's great pleasures, whether produced organically or not.

Data on the nutritional quality of organic foods isn't so firmly in favor of organic as taste data is. Perhaps the most appropriate thing that can be said is that many, many factors are involved in the production of food and that when it comes to the nutrient content of foods, the factor of organic production versus conventional approaches insignificance compared to the mountain of other factors such as the cultivar of fruit that you've selected, the amount of sun the plant received prior to harvest, the climate the plant was growing in, and the amount of water the plants received. Looking at specific nutrients such as protein, vitamin A, and vitamin B ends up becoming an exercise in futility. Some studies support the contention that organics are healthier, some studies support the contention that foods produced conventionally are healthier, and some studies show no difference between the two methods. Even beta-carotene, a vitamin "known" to be higher in fruits and vegetables produced organically, has been shown to be either higher or lower in organically grown foods, depending on the study you consult (Magkos, Arvaniti, and Zampelas 2003).

Contamination

There's been quite a bit of excitement among critics of organic foods regarding the possible presence of *Escherichia coli*, a bacterium that's potentially quite dangerous, in organic produce because of the use of manure in organic production. In a previous chapter I mentioned the care that must be taken with manure in order to reduce the risk of infesting food with this dangerous bacterium. Those who are concerned about the possibility of ingesting these bacteria in organic food should take note that current organic standards in the United States and the United Kingdom require organic growers to compost manure before using it to fertilize crops in such a way that *E. coli* contamination is highly unlikely. Still, although compost isn't likely to contaminate food with harmful bacteria, the use of compost or manure tea, because of the environment it provides for bacterial growth, could spread harmful bacteria.

Antioxidants

Perhaps the most realistic claim that organic growers can make is that organic production seems to increase the presence of certain chemicals, called antioxidants, that may be beneficial for people as a defense against cancer. A number of studies on the quantity of antioxidants in various organic fruits and vegetables have shown that this produce tends to have higher levels of these beneficial compounds than produce grown conventionally (Asami et al. 2003; Carbonaro et al. 2002). It's worth noting that one study found that food grown using something called sustainable agriculture, a system of growing food with reduced synthetic inputs (similar to

IPM) though not necessarily organic, had more antioxidants than even organically produced food. This is particularly noteworthy because those using sustainable practices could well be using synthetic fertilizers and/or pesticides (Asami et al. 2003).

People who regularly purchase organic food will be aware of the fact that often, and especially with locally grown food, a certain amount of insect damage is found. This damage is the result of a few things inherent to organic growing systems, including less reliance on pesticides, lower efficacy of organic pesticides, and higher tolerance for damage on produce before pesticides are applied. Although it makes fruits and vegetables look less attractive, insect and disease damage might actually be a good thing: it signals the affected plant to produce chemicals to defend itself, and by and large these chemicals are the very antioxidants that are considered beneficial in human diets.

What to do?

Organic farming isn't just using the right type of pesticides and fertilizers, it's also a way of life that many people embrace. This way of life includes growing plants in small plots and selling locally. Certainly some organic farms are large and industrialized, but most organic production is still local and accomplished by people who are good stewards of the land. Local produce may be more expensive than buying from the mass marketers, but buying this produce also supports a local economy. The visual quality of organic food is quite variable—sometimes local organic food looks great and sometimes it doesn't—but local organic produce is usually picked at a time closer to natural ripening than mass-produced food is, so its flavor is often better. If you're looking for a reason to buy organic food, this is it.

If you're looking for strong health or nutritional reasons to purchase organic food, you'll need to keep waiting. Despite the fact that papers are periodically published supporting this notion, the bulk of published research just doesn't support it. The increased presence of antioxidants in organic food is certainly a benefit, but conventionally grown food still contains these chemicals at a significant level, and if a food is grown using sustainable agricultural practices, something you won't generally find out by looking at the label, that food could well have more antioxidants than the same organic food.

If you're worried about synthetic pesticide residues, selecting organic foods for your table is an option, but really that's just trading one set of pesticides for another that's been less intensively researched. If you're really worried about pesticides on your food, you should research plants that are less likely to contain pesticides at all, such as onions, sweet corn, and sweet potatoes, select those for your dinner table, and wash your food well with hot water before eating it.

10

Conclusions

Organic growing started when people began to look at their world critically and evaluate why the earth became used up and less productive in the areas where they grew their crops. Over time they established that the problem was a loss of nutrients and of organic material to hold these nutrients in the soil. By adding organic materials such as compost back into the soil, we're adding nutrients and providing the soil with the matter it needs to make the ground a healthy place for plants. The heart of organic gardening, the spring from which it all flows, is healthy soil. Somehow, in some way, the term *organic gardening* has been transformed over time to mean so much more and yet so much less.

Organic gardening should be about making safe and smart choices, such as reducing the use of pesticides and increasing the use of mulches and compost. Instead it has come to mean making the natural choices, which includes many natural pesticides that may have significant problems. The natural choices aren't necessarily the wrong ones, but they're not necessarily the right choices either. All of us wish for a silver bullet: a pesticide that will kill all pests 100 percent of the time and be as safe as water for us and for other animals and beneficial insects. This pesticide doesn't exist and probably never will. In its absence we need to do our best to balance the safety of the pesticides we use with the likelihood that they'll be effective at controlling the problems we have in our gardens. If we start to divide pesticides by natural versus synthetic rather than by their safety and efficacy in controlling pests, we're just fooling ourselves into thinking that we're making rational decisions when in fact we're making a meaningless and artificial separation that could well be to our detriment.

I sometimes wonder what Rachel Carson would think if she saw what the organic movement has evolved into today. At some level I know she would be happy because those who garden and grow responsibly are starting to grasp the need for judicious use of pesticides and the need to understand what they apply. On another level, however, I think she would be disappointed as we continue to apply both organic and synthetic pesticides without a full understanding of their effects. What I hope she would appreciate is that doing things organically is a process and we're making our way toward a healthier future.

Bibliography

Aldwinckle, H. S., and R.P. Penev. 2004. Field evaluation of materials for control of fire blight infection of apple blossoms, 2003. *Fungicide and Nematicide Tests* 59: PF016.

Allen, T. C., R. J. Dicke, and H. H. Harris. 1944. Sabadilla, *Schoenocaulon* spp., with reference to its toxicity to houseflies. *Journal of Economic Entomology* 37: 400–407.

Ames, B. N., and L. S. Gold. 2000. Paracelsus to parascience: The environmental cancer distraction. *Mutation Research* 447: 3–13.

Ames, B. N., M. Profet, and L. S. Gold. 1990. Nature's chemicals and synthetic chemicals: Comparative toxicology. *Proceedings of the National Academy of Sciences of the United States of America* 87: 7782–7786.

Archer, T. E., and W. O. Gauer. 1979. Levels of cryolite on Thomson seedless grapes and raisins. 1979. *American Journal of Enology and Viticulture* 30 (3): 202–204.

Archer, V. E., and D. W. Jones. 2002. Capsaicin pepper, cancer, and ethnicity. *Medical Hypotheses* 59 (4): 450–457.

Asami, D. K., Y. J. Hong, D. M. Barrett, and A. E. Mitchell. 2003. Comparison of the total phenolic and ascorbic acid content of freeze-dried and air-dried marionberry, strawberry, and corn using conventional, organic, and sustainable agricultural practices. *Journal of Agricultural and Food Chemistry* 51 (5): 1237–1241.

Avery, D. T. 1995. *Saving the Planet with Pesticides and Plastics: The Environmental Triumph of High-Yield Farming.* Indianapolis, IN: Hudson Institute.

Baker, B. P., C. M. Benbrook, E. Groth III, and K. L. Benbrook. 2002. Pesticide residues in conventional, integrated pest management (IPM)-grown, and organic foods: Insights from three US data sets. *Food Additives and Contaminants* 19 (5): 427–446.

Balfour, E. 1943. *The Living Soil.* London: Faber and Faber.

Blokpoel, H. 1976. *Bird Hazards to Aircraft: Problems and Prevention of Bird-Aircraft Collision.* Toronto, Ontario, Canada: Clarke, Irwin and Company.

Boeke, S. J., M. G. Boersma, G. M. Alink, J.J.A. van Loon, A. van Huis, M. Dicke, and I.M.C.M. Rietjens. 2004. Safety evaluation of neem (*Azadirachta indica*) derived pesticides. *Journal of Ethnopharmacology* 94 (1): 25–41.

Brand, A. R., and P. P. Kellogg. 1939. Auditory responses of starlings, English sparrows, and domestic pigeons. *Wilson Bulletin* 51 (1): 38–41.

Brown, E., and B. Drees. 2002. Evaluation of "organic" and alternative imported fire ant mound drench treatments. Texas Imported Fire Ant Research and Management Project, http://fireants.tamu.edu.

Buckley, J. D., A. T. Meadows, M. E. Kadin, M. M. Le Beau, S. Siegel, and L. L. Robison. 2000. Pesticide exposures in children with non-Hodgkin's lymphoma. *Cancer* 89 (11): 2315–2321.

Burgel, K., C. Daniel, and E. Wyss. 2005. Effects of autumn kaolin treatments on the rosy apple aphid, *Dysaphis plantaginea* (Pass.) and possible modes of action. *Journal of Applied Entomology* 129 (6): 311–314.

Caboni, P., T. B. Sherer, N. Zhang, G. Taylor, H. M. Na, J. T. Greenamyre, and J. E. Casida. 2004. Rotenone, deguelin, their metabolites, and the rat model of Parkinson's disease. *Chemical Research in Toxicology* 17 (11): 1540–1548.

Calderon, F. J., L. E. Jackson, K. M. Scow, and D. E. Rolston. 2001. Short-term dynamics of nitrogen, microbial activity, and phospholipids fatty acids after tillage. *Soil Science Society of America Journal* 65 (1): 118–126.

Cantor, K. P., A. Blair, G. Everett, R. Gibson, L. F. Burmeister, L. M. Brown, L. Schuman, and F. R. Dick. 1992. Pesticides and other agricultural risk factors for non-Hodgkin's lymphoma among men in Iowa and Minnesota. *Cancer Research* 52: 2447–2455.

Carbonaro, M., M. Mattera, S. Nicoli, P. Bergamo, and M. Cappellone. 2002. Modulation of antioxidant compounds in organic vs. conventional fruit (peach, *Prunus persica* L., and pear, *Pyrus communis* L.). *Journal of Agricultural and Food Chemistry* 50: 5458–5462.

Carson, R. 1962. *Silent Spring.* New York: Houghton-Mifflin.

Cato, M. P., and M. T. Varro. 1967. *De Re Rustica.* Loeb Classical Library edition, translated by W. D. Hooper and H. B. Ash. London: Wm. Heinemann Ltd.

Chase, C. A., J. M. Scholberg, and G. E. MacDonald. 2004. Preliminary evaluation of nonsynthetic herbicides for weed management in organic orange production. *Proceedings of the Florida State Horticultural Society* 117: 135–138.

Colt, J. S., L. Stallones, L. L. Cameron, M. Dosemeci, and S. Uoar-Zahm. 2001. Proportionate mortality among U.S. migrant and seasonal farmworkers in twenty-four states. *American Journal of Industrial Medicine* 40: 604–611.

Conford, P. 2001. *The Origins of the Organic Movement.* Edinburgh, Scotland: Floris Books.

Curtis, P. D., I. A. Merwin, M. P. Pritts, and D. V. Peterson. 1994. Chemical repellents and plastic netting for reducing bird damage to sweet cherries, blueberries, and grapes. *HortScience* 29 (10): 1151–1155.

DeBach, P., and B. Bartlett. 1951. Effects of insecticides on biological control of insect pests of citrus. *Journal of Economic Entomology* 44: 372–383.

DeGregori, T. 2003. *The Origins of the Organic Agriculture Debate.* Ames, IA: Iowa State Press.

deNardo, E.A.B., and P. S. Grewal. 2003. Compatibility of *Steinernema feltiae* with pesticides and plant growth regulators used in glasshouse plant production. *Biocontrol Science and Technology* 13: 441–448.

De Roos, A. J., A. Blair, J. A. Rusiecki, J. A. Hoppin, M. Svec, M. Dosemeci, D. P. Sandler, and M. C. Alavanja. 2005. Cancer incidence among glyphosate-exposed pesticide applicators in agricultural health study. *Environmental Health Perspectictives* 113 (1): 49–54.

Dodd, J. C., and P. Jeffries. 1989. Effect of fungicides on three vesicular-arbuscular mycorrhizal fungi associated with winter wheat (*Triticum aestivum* L.). *Biology and Fertility of Soils* 7 (2): 120–128.

Dudderar, G. R., S. Tellman, and D. E. Elshoff. 1997. The effectiveness of a new mole repellent for preventing damage to lawns by Eastern voles. *Proceedings of the Eastern Wildlife Management Conference* 7: 149–152.

Duffy, B., C. Sarreal, S. Ravva, and S. Stanker. 2004. Effect of molasses on regrowth of *E. coli* O157:H7 and salmonella in compost teas. *Compost Science and Utilization* 12 (1): 93–96.

Enders, L. 1868. Ueber die ermittelung fremder bitterstoffe in dem biere, namentlich derjenigen der quassia, des bitterklee's und wermuth's. *Arch. Pharm.* R. 2, Bd. 135, Heft 3: 209–224.

Epstein, L., and S. Bassein. 2001. Pesticide applications of copper on perennial crops in California, 1993 to 1998. *Journal of Environmental Quality* 30: 1844–1847.

Finch, S., H. Billiald, and R. H. Collier. 2003. Companion planting—Do aromatic plants disrupt host-plant finding by the cabbage root fly and the onion fly more effectively than non-aromatic plants? *Entomologia Experimentalis et Applicata* 109: 183–195.

Flint, H. M., N. J. Parks, J. E. Holmes, J. A. Jones, and C. M. Higuera. 1995. Tests of garlic oil for control of the silverleaf whitefly, *Bemesia argentifollii* Bellows and Perring, in cotton. *Southwestern Entomological Society* 20: 137–150.

Garabrant, D. H., and M. A. Philbert. 2002. Review of 2,4-Dichlorophen-oxyacetic acid (2,4-D) epidemiology and toxicology. *Critical Reviews in Toxicology* 32 (4): 233–257.

Gillman, J. H. 2006. *The Truth about Garden Remedies: What Works, What Doesn't & Why.* Portland, OR: Timber Press.

Gold, L. S., T. H. Slone, B. R. Stern, N. B. Manley, and B. N. Ames. 1992. Rodent carcinogens: Setting priorities. *Science* 258: 261–265.

Gordon, F. C., and D. A. Potter. 1985. Efficiency of Japanese beetle (Coleoptera: Scarabaeidae) traps in reducing defoliation of plants in the urban landscape and effect on larval density in turf. *Journal of Economic Entomology* 78: 774–778.

———. 1986. Japanese beetle (Coleoptera: Scarabaeidae) traps: Evaluation of single and multiple arrangements for reducing defoliation of plants in urban landscape. *Journal of Economic Entomology* 79: 1381–1384.

Gordon, R. C. 1985. The Coccinellidae (Coleoptera) of America North of Mexico. *Journal of the New York Entomological Society* 93 (1): 1–912.

Griffith, R. 1847. *Medical Botany, or Descriptions of the More Important Plants Used in Medicine.* Philadelphia, PA: Lee and Blanchard.

Griffiths, R. E. 1988. Efficacy testing of ultrasonic bird repellers. In *Vertebrate Pest Control and Management Materials*, vol. 5, ed. R. W. Bullard and S. A. Shumake, 56–63. Philadelphia, PA: American Society for Testing and Materials.

Groth, D. E., and C. A. Martinson. 1983. Increased endomycorrhizal infection of maize and soybean after soil treatment and metalaxyl. *Plant Disease* 67: 1377–1378.

Gupta, P., and M. R. Siddiqui. 1999. Compatibility studies on *Steinernema carpocapsae* with some pesticidal chemicals. *Indian Journal of Entomology* 61: 220–225.

Hardell, L., and Eriksson, M. 1999. A case-control study of non-Hodgkin lymphoma and exposure to pesticides. *Cancer* 85 (6): 1353–1360.

Hatterman-Valenti, H., M.D.K. Owen, and N. E. Christians. 1996. Ground ivy (*Glechoma hederacea* L.) control in a Kentucky blue turfgrass with borax. *Journal of Environmental Horticulture* 14 (2): 101–104.

Hayes, T. B., A. Collins, M. Lee, M. Mendoza, N. Noriega, A. A. Stuart, and A. Vonk. 2002. Hermaphroditic, demasculinized frogs after exposure to the herbicide atrazine at low ecologically relevant doses. *Proceedings of the National Academy of Sciences of the United States of America* 99 (8): 5476–5480.

Held, D. W., P. Gonsiska, and D. A. Potter. 2003. Evaluating planting and non-host masking odors for protecting roses from the Japanese beetle. *Journal of Environmental Entomology* 96 (1): 81–87.

Holb, I. J., P. F. De Jong, and B. Heijne. 2003. Efficacy and phytotoxicity of lime sulphur in organic apple production. *Annals of Applied Biology* 142: 225–233.

Holland, P. T., D. Hamilton, B. Ohlin, and M. W. Skidmore. 1994. Effects of storage and processing on pesticide residues in plant products. *Pure and Applied Chemistry* 66 (2): 335–356.

Hollingsworth, R. G., and J. W. Armstrong. 2003. Effectiveness of products containing metaldehyde, copper, or extracts of yucca or neem for control of *Zonitoides arboreus* (Say), a snail pest of orchid roots in Hawaii. *International Journal of Pest Control* 49 (2): 115–122.

Hori, M. 1996. Settling inhibition and insecticidal activity of garlic and onion oils against *Myzus persicae* (Suzler). *Applied Entomology and Zoology* 31: 605–612.

Howard, A. 1940. *An Agricultural Testament*. New York: Oxford University Press.

Howard, L. O. 1900. *Notes on the Mosquitos of the United States*. Bulletin 25, U.S. Department of Agriculture, Division of Entomology.

Huang, H., Z. Smilowitz, and M. Saunders. 1995. Toxicity and field efficacy of cryolite against Colorado potato beetle (Coleoptera: Chrysomelidae) larvae. *Journal of Economic Entomology* 88 (5): 1408–1414.

Huang, Y., S. X. Chen, and S. H. Ho. 2000. Bioactivities of methyl allyl disulfide and diallyl trisulfide from essential oil of garlic to two species of stored-product pests, *Sitophilus zeamais* and *Tribolium castaneum*. *Journal of Economic Entomology* 93: 537–543.

Hygnstrom, S. E., and S. R. Craven. 1988. Electric fences and commercial repellents for reducing deer damage in cornfields. *Wildlife Society Bulletin* 16: 291–296.

Ibrahim, M. A., P. Kainulainen, A. Aflatuni, K. Tiilikkala, and J. K. Holopainen. 2001. Insecticidal, repellent, antimicrobial activity and phytotoxicity of essential oils: With special reference to limonene and its suitability for control of insect pests. *Agricultural and Food Science in Finland* 10: 243–259.

Jabaji-Hare, S. H., and W. B. Kendrick. 1987. Response of an endomycorrhizal fungus in *Allium porrum* L. to differentiate concentrations of the systemic fungicide metalaxyl (Ridomil) and fosetyl-Al (Aliette). *Soil Biology and Biochemistry* 19: 95–99.

James, L. F., K. E. Panter, W. Gaffield, and R. J. Molyneux. 2004. Biomedical applications of poisonous plant research. *Journal of Agricultural and Food Chemistry* 52: 3211–3230.

Jauron, R. 1997. Borax on ground ivy: Boon or bane? *Horticulture and Home Pest News* (Iowa State University), August 22, 132–133.

Katan, J. 1981. Solar heating (solarization) of soil for control of soilborne pests. *Annual Review of Phytopathology* 19: 211–236.

Katan, J., G. Fishler, and A. Grinstein. 1980. Solar heating of the soil and other methods for the control of Fusarium, additional soilborne pathogens, and weeds in cotton. *Proceedings of the Fifth International Congress of the Mediterranean Phytopathology Union*, 80–81.

Kenrick, W. 1833. *The New American Orchardist*. Boston, MA: Otis, Broaders, and Company.

Kinsey, C. L. 1976. Tests of two deer barrier forms. *Minnesota Wildlife Research Quarterly* 36: 122–138.

Kovach, J., C. Petzoldt, J. Degni, and J. Tette. 1992. A method to measure the environmental impact of pesticides. *New York's Food and Life Sciences Bulletin*. Geneva, NY: New York State Agricultural Experiment Station, Cornell University. http://nysipm.cornell.edu/publications/eiq/default.asp

Kudva, I. T., K. Blanch, and C. J. Hovde. 1998. Analysis of *Escherichia coli* O157:H7 survival in ovine or bovine manure and manure slurry. *Applied and Environmental Microbiology* 64 (9): 3166–3174.

Lemieux, N. C., B. K. Maynard, and W. A. Johnson. 2000. Evaluation of commercial deer repellents on ornamentals in nurseries. *Journal of Environmental Horticulture* 18: 5–8.

Lindsay, J. 1794. An account of the *quassia polygama*, or bitter-wood of Jamaica. *Transcripts of the Royal Society of Edinburgh* 3 (8): 205–214.

Lodeman, E. G. 1906. *The Spraying of Plants*. New York: Macmillan.

MacCollom, C., C. Lauzon, E. Payne, and W. Currier. 1994. Apple maggot (Diptera: Tephritidae) trap enhancement with washed bacterial cells. *Environmental Entomology* 23 (2): 354–359.

Madanlar, N., Z. Yoldas, E. Durmusoglu, and A. Gul. 2002. Investigations on the natural pesticides against pests in vegetable greenhouses in Izmir (Turkey). *Turkiye Entomoloji Dergisi* 26: 181–195.

Maele-Fabry, G. V., and J. L. Willems. 2003. Occupation-related pesticide exposure and cancer of the prostate: A meta-analysis. *Occupational and Environmental Medicine* 60: 634–642.

Magkos, F., F. Arvaniti, and A. Zampelas. 2003. Organic food: Nutritious food or food for thought? A review of the evidence. *International Journal of Food Sciences and Nutrition* 54 (5): 357–371.

Majule, A. E., C. P. Topper, and S. Nortcliff. 1997. The environmental effects of dusting cashew (*Anacardium occidentale* L.) trees with sulfur in Southern Tanzania. *Tropical Agriculture* 74 (1): 25–33.

Malamy, J., and D. F. Kessig. 1992. Salicylic acid and plant disease resistance. *The Plant Journal* 2: 643–654.

Massey, L. M. 1925. A cautionary word about fungicides. *The American Rose Annual* 10: 89–92.

McGovern, R. J., M. Hoffine, D. S. Myers, T. A. Davis, and T. E. Seijo. 2003. Field evaluation of fungicides for control of black spot in rose, 2002. *Fungicide and Nematicide Tests* Report No. 58: OT047.

McIndoo, N. E., and A. F. Sievers. 1917. Quassia extract as a contact insecticide. *Journal of Agricultural Research* 10 (10): 497–530.

McIndoo, N. E., A. F. Sievers, and W. S. Abbott. 1919. Derris as an insecticide. *Journal of Agricultural Research* 17: 177–200.

McLennan, J. A., N.P.E. Langham, and R.E.R. Porter. 1995. Deterrent effect of eye-spot balls on birds. *New Zealand Journal of Crop and Horticultural Science* 23 (2): 139–144.

Meisenheimer, T. M., M. Lund, E. M. Baker, and J. W. Suttie. 1994. Biochemical basis of warfarin and bromadiolone resistance in the house mouse, *Mus musculus domesticus*. *Biochemical Pharmacology* 47 (4): 673–678.

Mulrooney, R. P. 2003. Evaluation of biorational fungicides for control of black spot of rose, 2002. *Fungicide and Nematicide Tests* Report No. 58: OT035.

Nakamura, K., Y. Shirota, T. Kaneko, and S. Matsuoka. 1995. Scaring effectiveness of eyespot balloons on the rufous turtle dove, *Streptopelia orientalis* (Latham), in a flight cage. *Applied Entomology and Zoology* 30 (3): 383–392.

Nelson, H., ed. 1975. *Pyrethrum Flowers*. St. Paul, MN: BMC Graphic Arts Services.

Newsome, W. H., and J. B. Shields. 1980. Residues of rotenone and rotenolone on lettuce and tomato fruit after treatment in the field with rotenone formulations. *Journal of Agricultural and Food Chemistry* 28: 722–724.

Ostrom, G. S. 1994. Cryolite results unexpected. CATI publication 940701.

California Agricultural Technology Institute, Viticulture and Enology Research Center.

Ottoboni, M. Alice. 1997. *The Dose Makes the Poison.* New York: Wiley.

Paarman, P. M. 1779. Examen ligni quassiae. In T. L. Wittwer, ed., *Delectus Dissertationum Medacarum Argentoratensium* 3: 35–66.

Papaioannou-Souliotis, P., D. Markoyiannaki-Printziou, A. Tsagkarakou, I. Rumbos, and I. Adamopoulos. 1998. Effects of different fungicides and insecticides on populations of *Phytoseius finitimus* (Ribaga) in vineyard in four regions of Greece. *Redia* 81: 17–35.

Patt, J. M., G. C. Hamilton, and J. H. Lashomb. 1997. Foraging success of parasitoid wasps on flowers: Interplay of insect morphology, floral architecture, and searching behavior. *Entomologia Experimentalis et Applicata* 83 (1): 21–30.

Pliny. 1971. *Natural History*, Books 17–19. Loeb Classical Library edition, trans. H. Rackham. London: Wm. Heinemann Ltd.

Porter, W. F. 1983. A baited electric fence for controlling deer damage to orchard seedlings. *Wildlife Society Bulletin* 11: 325–327.

Quy, R. J., D. P. Cowan, C. V. Prescott, J. E. Gill, G. M. Kerins, G. Dunsford, A. Jones, and A. D. MacNicoll. 1995. Control of a population of Norway rats resistant to anticoagulant rodenticides. *Pesticide Science* 45 (3): 283–295.

Rankin, M. A., and S. Rankin. 1980. Some factors affecting presumed migratory flight activity of the convergent ladybeetle *Hippodamia convergens. Biological Bulletin* 158: 356–369.

Raupp, M., R. Webb, A. Szczepaniec, D. Booth, and R. Ahern. 2004. Incidence, abundance, and severity of mites on hemlocks following applications of imidacloprid. *Journal of Arboriculture* 30 (2): 108–113.

Redmond, C., and D. Potter. 1995. Lack of efficacy of in-vitro and putatively in-vitro produced *Bacillus popilliae* against field populations of Japanese beetle (Coleoptera: Scarabaeidae) grubs in Kentucky. *Journal of Economic Entomology* 88: 846–854.

Relyea, R. A. 2005. The impact of insecticides and herbicides on the biodiversity and productivity of aquatic communities. *Ecological Applications* 15: 618–627.

Riotte, L. 1998. *Carrots Love Tomatoes: Secrets of Companion Planting for Successful Gardening*, 2nd ed. North Adams, MA: Storey.

Roark, R. C. 1947. Some promising insecticidal plants. *Economic Botany* 1: 437–445.

Rodale, J. I. 1948. *The Organic Front.* Emmaus, PA: Rodale Press.

Rovesti, L., T. Fiorini, G. Bettini, E. W. Heinzpeter, and F. Tagliente. 1990. Compatibility of *Steinernema* spp. and *Heterorhabditis* spp. with pesticides. *Informatore Fitopatologico* 40 (9): 55–61.

Ryan, J. J., J. C. Pilon, and R. Leduc. 1982. Composite sampling in the determination of pyrethrins in fruit samples. *Journal of the Association of Official Analytical Chemists* 65: 904–908.

Scheuerell, S. J., and W. F. Mahaffee. 2004. Compost tea as a container medium drench for suppressing seedling damping-off caused by *Pythium ultimum*. *Phytopathology* 94 (11): 1156–1163.

Schilder, A.M.C., J. M. Gillett, and R. W. Sysak. 2004. Evaluation of fungicides for control of foliar and fruit diseases of strawberry, 2003. *Fungicide and Nematicide Tests* Report No. 59: SMF030.

Smil, V. 2001. *Enriching the Earth: Fritz Haber, Carl Bosch, and the Transformation of World Food Production*. Cambridge, MA: MIT Press.

Smith, S., and V. Krischik. 1999. Effects of systemic imidacloprid on *Coleomegilla maculate* (Coleoptera: Coccinellidae). *Environmental Entomology* 28 (6): 1189–1195.

Speiser, B., and C. Kistler. 2001. Field tests with a molluscicide containing iron phosphate. *Crop Protection* 21: 389–394.

Stevens, G. R., and L. Clark. 1998. Bird repellents: Development of avian-specific tear gases for resolution of human-wildlife conflicts. *International Biodeterioration and Biodegradation* 42 (2/3): 153–160.

Stier, J. C. 1999. Corn gluten meal and other natural products for weed control in turfgrass. *Wisconsin Fertilizer, Aglime and Pest Management Conference Proceedings*. http://www.soils.wisc.edu/extension/FAPM/proceedings/4C.stier.pdf

Stoll, G. 1988. *Natural Crop Protection in the Tropics*. Filderstadt, Germany: Margraf.

Sundin, G. W., and G. R. Ehret. 2004. Fire blight control on Jonathan apple in 2003. *Fungicide and Nematicide Tests* Report No. 59: PF007.

Thompson, G. D., S. H. Hutchins, and T. C. Sparks. 1999. Development of spinosad and attributes of a new class of insect control products. In *Radcliffe's IPM World Textbook*, ed. E. B. Radcliffe and W. D. Hutchison. St. Paul, MN: University of Minnesota. http://ipmworld.umn.edu

Triebskorn, R., K. Christensen, and L. Heim. 1998. Effect of orally and dermally applied metaldehyde on mucus cells of slugs (*Deroceras reticulatum*) depending on temperature and duration of exposure. *Journal of Molluscan Studies* 64: 467–487.

Unruh, T. R., A. L. Knight, J. Upton, D. M. Glenn, and G. J. Puterka. 2000.

Particle films for suppression of the codling moth (Lepidoptera: Tortricidae) in apple and pear orchards. *Journal of Economic Entomology* 93 (3): 737–743.

U.S. Environmental Protection Agency. 1996. Microbial Pesticide Test Guidelines, OPPTS 885.0001. Overview for Microbial Pest Control Agents, EPA 712-C-96-280.

Vincent, C., and M. J. Lareau. 1993. Effectiveness of methiocarb and netting for bird control in a highbush blueberry plantation in Quebec, Canada. *Crop Protection* 12 (5): 397–399.

Vonier, P. M., D. A. Crain, J. A. McLachlan, L. J. Guillette, Jr., and S. F. Arnold. 1996. Interaction of environmental chemicals with the estrogen and progesterone receptors from the oviduct of the American alligator. *Environmental Health Perspectives* 104 (12): 1318–1323.

Weeden, C., A. Shelton, Y. Li, and M. Hoffman, eds. 2006. *Bacillus popilliae* (Eubacteriales: Bacillaceae). In *Biological Control: A Guide to Natural Enemies in North America*. Ithaca, NY: Cornell University. http://www.nysaes.cornell.edu/ent/biocontrol/pathogens

Werner, S. J., H. J. Homan, M. L. Avery, G. M. Linz, E. A. Tillman, A. A. Slowik, R. W. Byrd, T. M. Primus, and M. J. Goodall. 2005. Evaluation of Bird Shield as a blackbird repellent in ripening rice and sunflower fields. *Wildlife Society Bulletin* 33 (1): 251–257.

White, R. F. 1979. Acetylsalicylic acid (aspirin) induces resistance to tobacco mosaic virus in tobacco. *Virology* 99: 410–412.

Wiener, J. G., and M. H. Smith. 1972. Relative efficiencies of four small mammal traps. *Journal of Mammalogy* 53 (4): 868–873.

Witmer, G. A., A. A. Hakim, and B. W. Moser. 2000. Investigations of methods to reduce damage by voles. *The Ninth Wildlife Damage Management Conferences Proceedings*, 357–365.

Woronecki, P. P. 1988. Effect of ultrasonic, visual, and sonic devices on pigeon numbers in a vacant building. *Proceedings of the Thirteenth Vertebrate Pest Conference* 13: 266–272.

Zahm, S. H., and A. Blair. 1992. Pesticides and non-Hodgkin's lymphoma. *Cancer Research* (Supplement) 52: 5485s–5488s

Zang, X., E. K. Fukuda, and J. D. Rosen. 1998. Multiresidue analytical procedure for insecticides used by organic farmers. *Journal of Agricultural Food Chemistry* 46: 2206–2210.

Zörnig, H. 1909. *Arzneidrogen alz nachschlagebuch für den Gobrauch der Apotheker, Ärze, Veterinararze, Drogisten und Studierenden der Pharmazie*. Leipzig, Germany: W. Klinkhardt.

Index